The Deepest Longing
of
Young People

The Deepest Longing of Young People

Loving Without Conditions

Jerry Goebel

Saint Mary's Press®

I read this book with something approaching awe. It is so full of compassion for young people, so eminently practical, and written with such heartfelt passion that you cannot help yourself from saying, "There is truth here."

For more than thirty years Jerry Goebel has been working with young people in gangs, juvenile detention centers, and prisons, and his philosophy can be summed up in just a few words: Listen thoroughly, and speak only when you know the right questions to ask. This same philosophy of life has been stated by spiritual teachers in different ways throughout the ages, and Jerry's book is a potent reminder of the need to listen with an open heart and mind.

Every parent and everyone who works with youth should read this book.

—Katherine Ketcham, coauthor of *Teens Under the Influence*

 Genuine recycled paper with 10% post-consumer waste. 5116600

The publishing team included Laurie Delgatto, development editor; Lorraine Kilmartin, reviewer; prepress and manufacturing coordinated by the prepublication and production services departments of Saint Mary's Press.

Printed in the United States of America

Printing: 9 8 7 6 5 4 3 2 1

Year: 2014 13 12 11 10 09 08 07 06

ISBN-13: 978-0-88489-935-8
ISBN-10: 0-88489-935-7

Library of Congress Cataloging-in-Publication Data

Goebel, Jerry.
    The deepest longing of young people : loving without conditions / Jerry Goebel.
        p. cm.
    ISBN-13: 978-0-88489-935-8 (pbk.)
    ISBN-10: 0-88489-935-7 (pbk.)
    1. Church work with youth. 2. Love—Religious aspects—Christianity. 3. God—Love. I. Title.
    BV4447.G585 2006
    259'.2—dc22

                                                        2006008448

Dedication

This book is filled with stories. They are stories of real young people, and most of the stories took place while I was writing this book. Every story is a cluster of hurt, abandonment, and finally, hope. Every story is a poignant reminder that we still haven't taken the Gospel to the ends of the earth—or even to our own neighborhoods.

One particular story talks about a map of my city that shows the reports of child abuse as dots in yellow and red. "It's like our town has the chicken pox," said a friend.

This book is dedicated to every young person attached to each story within these pages; it is also dedicated to the many dots of yellow and red that we have yet to reach.

I dedicate it to the mentors who so faithfully work with me. I also dedicate it to the staff at Walla Walla County Juvenile Detention Facility, who work so hard to bring hope to each story and every yellow or red dot that they encounter.

"God, make us authentic . . . to them."

Author Acknowledgments

I want to thank my family, who, for the last few months, tiptoed around my closet while I typed away in reclusive silence (with the exception of a few artistic outbursts).

I also want to sincerely thank Laurie Delgatto, my editor, throughout this lengthy process. Laurie, thank you for your wonderful gift of keeping me focused; you may be receiving multiple phone calls from others who would like your secret.

Finally, I don't know if this is customary, but I really wish to thank God, whose presence I felt in a very personal way during this process. I realize what an honor it is to have the opportunity to share what you believe . . . and even more to be able to incorporate what you believe into one's daily life. Like Francis of Assisi, I want to open each day and close each evening with the delicious prayer: "My dearest God, who are you? And, who am I but your useless servant?"

Thank you, dearest God, for this opportunity.

Contents

Foreword

As fate would have it, I'm on tour for one of my own books as I write the foreword to this one. A close friend is traveling with me, and the two of us have been reading Jerry's book together. It has become the devotional for this journey, a road trip of hamburgers and coffee cups, deep questions and reflections.

I have not always been a writer, and I miss some things about my old life. I used to spend my mornings talking to people, making phone calls—connecting. Now I go into a quiet room, shut the door, and spend my time alone in worlds of my own making. It's hard to close the door, to feel your sense of community slipping. People stop calling you.

I share this odd bit of information with you because you've picked up a book that was written by a writer, someone who by his very nature must find vast stretches of time to be completely alone. What I've learned from Jerry—who lives in my town—is that being a writer is no excuse for being a disconnected member of my community. The book you are about to read took a lot of time to write, but it didn't stop Jerry from serving people each and every afternoon while he was busy getting in his two thousand words a day. The people came first, the words followed. This is a lesson I needed to learn.

I sometimes go through periods of time when I can't find any meaning in the ancient words of the Bible. I read them, then read them again, then go for a run and try to think happy thoughts. It's a problem. The wonderful thing is that God honors my effort with moments of clarity. Jerry's book is chock full of moments of clarity—those times when you read an explanation of a passage and in a flash you're changed. You understand. It's hard to find books that teach hard lessons and challenge me to change. This book accomplished both.

Jerry and I share a mutual friend who spends a lot of time visiting prisoners at the Washington State Penitentiary. It's a pretty rough place. I asked our friend why he chose to go to the prison and meet with some of the men there, and he told me that it was in the prison where he found Jesus. It makes sense when you think about it. If you go to the same kinds of places Jesus did, it's more likely that you'll find him there. It's this observation, if none other, that should give you encouragement to read this book. It came out of a daily life of service. It was born and nurtured and raised in a juvenile center. The fingerprints of Jesus are all over it.

There were a hundred times in my reading of this book when I was given that rare and wonderful gift—the gift of feeling that Jesus was talking to me, calling me close, moving me to examine myself, my motives, my values. This book is full of the best kind of hard teaching. It's made me rethink my values.

I learned one other thing between cups of coffee and getting lost as I read Jerry's book, and maybe it's the most important thing of all. If you're looking for a way to change young people, then this book is probably not a very good choice. If, on the other hand, you want to understand how to change yourself so that you can minister to young people in your community, then you now hold a treasure in your hand. It is that change, and the blessing that comes with it, that makes it possible to heal a broken world. What more can we ask for from a book?

Patrick Carman
Author of the Land of Elyon series
September 13, 2005

1 This Is My Beloved

And when Jesus had been baptized, just as he came up from the water, suddenly the heavens were opened to him and he saw the Spirit of God descending like a dove and alighting on him. And a voice from heaven said, "This is my Son, the Beloved, with whom I am well pleased." (Matthew 3:16–17)

This book is about the greatest hunger in our hearts, a hunger so deep it gnaws at us daily and longs to be fed. This book is about the only love that can fill that hunger and lead to the purest joy that we were destined to know—both in this life and eternally. Within these pages, I hope you will find the knowledge—but even more importantly—the power to live out the Great News of Jesus Christ, to be blessed as he was blessed, and to love like he loved.

My prayer is that this book will enrich the conversations you have with God, but also with those around you, empowering you to name (and help young people name) their most significant values and how naming those values can help protect the young people you care for from being manipulated by others or distracted by a false happiness that would steal their integrity. This book is about passing on the greatest blessing that God desires to give to every life; it is what I simply refer to as the "beloved blessing."

I Am So Wonderfully Pleased with You!

It is hard to embrace the idea that the same God who created the universe, who changed chaos into order, who painted the sky with stars and stirred the deep waters with life, that this breathtaking God was also a great parent. God raised a child who made himself completely available to serve others, who cast aside his own will to become the perfect sacrifice, and to embrace us while we were yet sinners. Could we imagine becoming so strong in our faith that nothing could dampen our love of God, nothing could steal our joy, and nothing could distract us from our core values? That is the first part of "becoming the blessing," when we accept the name "beloved."

As we look at our heavenly parent and see how our God raised Jesus, we can see important clues into how God wants us to transition into beloved and blessing. The first time we see God speak directly to Jesus (in front of witnesses) is when God gives Jesus the "beloved blessing" of the Jordan (see Matthew 3:16–17). There, Jesus abandons his career as a respected craftsman of Nazareth and the comfort of his earthly family's home, and becomes totally available to the call of God. It is at that very moment that the heavens part and God's holy voice lifts in blessing, "This is my Son, the Beloved, with whom I am well pleased."

Here is eternity's most marvelous blessing, a blessing that every man, woman, and child has longed to hear since the day of our creation: "I love you so very much, I am so wonderfully pleased with you."

How I wish we could only understand how much pain and suffering is caused in the lives of our young people by the absence of this beloved blessing. If we would even taste that pain, we would want nothing more from life than to run from door to door trying to insure that every child would hear and understand the wealth and beauty of the beloved blessing. We would want every young person we know to experience the richness of those words: "I love you so very much, I am so wonderfully pleased with you."

If I had to pinpoint what truly fills our streets and jails with defeat, breaks down relationships, and binds shame and hatred to broken lives, it would be the lack of this beloved blessing.

This book emphasizes how accepting that blessing can translate into becoming a blessing to all those around us, especially the young people we minister to and with. Accepting the name "beloved" is the first part of God's gift; becoming the blessing is the second. We could impart this blessing to an entire future generation if we could just embrace the title "beloved" ourselves. All young people desperately need both aspects of the beloved blessing if they are going to become mature, faithful adults.

Imagine the fulfillment in the lives of those around us if we could bless them like God blessed Jesus? Imagine offering young people an unconditional blessing, not based upon what they will someday have or do but based instead upon who they are in the eyes of the one whom Jesus called Daddy. Imagine the strength we could give young people if they knew that their belovedness was not based upon the approval or rejection of their peers, or even the comforts or stability of the world around them. Imagine how resilient those young people would be if they were able to call upon this beloved blessing in the midst of feeling peer rejection, making difficult life decisions, or trying to remain compassionate in a harsh and chaotic world.

What God blessed on that incredible day was Jesus's willingness to set his needs aside and become a servant to all.

It was the free decision that Jesus made to make himself utterly available to do God's will—whatever the circumstances, whatever the costs. The blessing of God was not based upon the accomplishments of Jesus but instead upon his availability to be God's servant.

It is also imperative that we understand that God's blessing does not lead to personal comfort in our Lord's life. In fact, the blessing results in Jesus being *led* (which literally means "arrested") by the Holy Spirit and delivered to the desert for intense testing by Satan (see Matthew 4:1). Jesus is not blessed for a life of leisure but for a life of self-sacrifice and service.

From Cursed to Blessing

Our world offers so many false blessings to our young people. They are the false blessings of Satan who constantly badgered Jesus, "If God really loved you (if you are the Messiah), then prove it." "If you really are God's beloved, then do this. . . ." When Satan finds that deception is impotent against our Lord, he switches tactics and says, "All right, if you will worship me, then you can have anything you want."

How often do young people hear that false blessing in their own lives—and are fooled into thinking it is the real thing. "I will love you if . . ." "The more you have or do, the more important you are." It is a false blessing based upon having or doing but not upon being. God, the compassionate Father, blesses us for being his beloved children. (We will explore this in more detail in chapter 5.)

To bless like God blessed takes unparalleled maturity. Many adults in our society simply don't have the blessing themselves, let alone the capacity to offer such deep unselfish love to young people. But you and I—together—we will change that. We can stop that progression even if it has always been a part of our own inheritance. We can change from a lack of blessing in our lives to becoming a fountain of blessing to the young—indeed, to our communities.

Earlier this week I sat with fourteen of our mentors and fourteen incarcerated youth, and we talked about being "accepted without conditions" (the beloved blessing). These young people's lives are so filled with rejection and violence that I now realize those characteristics are the lenses through which they view their world. One young lady named Kelly spoke of her mom's anger on the day Kelly had finally realized that she too was named "beloved of God." Her mother cursed Kelly and shouted, "Does this mean you aren't going to do heroin with me anymore?"

As we spoke about acceptance without conditions, Kelly said, "I don't think that my mom will ever accept me like that, but I think I can finally accept her without any conditions."

Kelly has now become the blessing of God. Despite being cursed, she has become a beloved blesser. God has moved into her heart and expanded it beyond the incapacitating boundaries of this world's anger, hurt, and rejection. She now holds the key to a blessing that no one will ever be able to take from her.

Isn't that what we want for all our young people? Isn't that what we long for ourselves? Isn't that the beloved blessing we so desire for all the Kellys of our world to carry with them throughout their lives? from heroin user to follower of Christ. from incarcerated to freed. from cursed to blessed.

We can help young people become beloved blessers and, in the end, this is the only blessing that is truly enduring and empowering. For even if daily we tell young people how wonderful they are and that we love them—that they are lovable—until they are able to love and bless others, they will never know they are loved. Until that point they are like bottomless cups and no matter how much love we pour into them, the cup will always be empty. We are beloved and we can bless. That's the commission of God to Jesus. That is the blessing God longs—even delights—to pass on to all of us and to all our Kellys.

The beloved blessing is the bottom to our cup. To truly experience the awareness that God is "well pleased" with us is the first step to being able to overflow with that blessing onto the lives of this generation.

> Give, and it will be given to you, A good measure, pressed down, shaken together, running over, will be put into your lap, for the measure you give will be the measure you get back. (Luke 6:38)

Blessed Are Your Circumstances

For over three decades, I have worked with church youth, street youth, and incarcerated youth; with youth ministers, teachers, and parents; I have traveled all over the world asking groups and individuals some variation of the following question: "Are you leading young people in such a way that you will pass on God's most important values to them?"

Let's break that question down into two components:

- What does God want (or value) for you to teach to the young people you lead?
- Are you modeling a lifestyle that will help young people recognize that vision?

The generation preceding us might have responded to that first question by saying, "We want our children to be better off than we were." But I hear a different cry from this generation of parents, ministers, and educators. Today, I hear parents say they want happiness for their children, and when asked what they mean by *happiness,* I hear them say words like *well-being, balance, joy,* and even *blessed.*

But do we understand what we mean by *blessed?*

To the Hebrew people, a blessing was the greatest gift a father would ever give to his first-born son (the Hebrew culture was very patriarchic). In the blessing, the eldest son received the right to the family name. It was the legal authority to lead the tribe and make covenants with other tribes. Once given, the blessing could never be taken away!

However, the word for *blessing* was much richer than personal happiness; to be blessed was to be given the responsibility of the whole tribe—the "house of God." In fact, that was the first term for church. The church was a nomadic people on a journey—not a building or a place. The blessing was always communal and never individual.

Christ uses two words for *blessing* (when translated into Greek). The first word, *makarios,* is circumstantial, it is like our word *happiness* and is akin to the word *luck* or *happenstance.* This blessing happens to you; it is not something you make, but rather something that you are given. It would be like saying, "Blessed are your circumstances." The second word is *eulogeo.* (We will talk more about this word in the "Blessed Are Your Choices" section.)

Luke tells us that Jesus takes the Apostles aside and gives them a very personal message about the pathway to the Kingdom of God (see Luke 6:17–49). Jesus intimately calls the disciples around him and shares with them the blessed attitudes of being in the Kingdom of God. These words were not yet meant for the crowds. The Apostles had just left everything (including their largest catch of fish) sitting on the shores of the Sea of Galilee in order to follow an itinerant rabbi. However, in exchange for their radical availability, they literally see the Kingdom of heaven begin to flower around them in the healing of the crippled, the blind, and the lame who are touched by the beloved child of God. As a result of their availability to Jesus, they are told:

> Blessed are you who are poor,
>   for yours is the kingdom of God.

(Luke 6:20)

Because they had left everything behind to follow Jesus, because they even became poor to follow him, they are blessed by their circumstances. Christ tells them they should be happy—because they were allowed to be among the first to witness the revelation of God's Kingdom.

Blessed Are Your Choices

The other word for blessing is *eulogeo* (as in *eulogy*). Most of us might think of a eulogy as a ten-minute summary given by the officiate of a funeral. That brief ten minutes (or less) can summarize decades of a person's time on earth. In essence, a eulogy says, "Here were this person's circumstances, and this is what he or she chose to do with them." This is *eulogeo.*

When we say we want our young people to be blessed, isn't *eulogeo* the type of blessing we desire for them? Don't we want them to know they can be blessed, they can find joy—even choose it—in spite of what is happening in the world around them? To be faithful, mature adults, we must learn to self-initiate joy, self-initiate love, and self-initiate change—and it is an ability both adults and children in our society sorely lack.

To self-initiate joy in our lives requires that we move from waiting for others to feed our emotions to taking the initiative to name our values and pursue them. Like the disciples, we are no longer in the audience, we are in the game. We must take personal responsibility for the lack of joy or love in our lives.

So often I hear kids tell me the reason they committed a crime or took drugs was, "I was bored." This is the primary sin of an "entertain-me culture." Adults and children alike wait for joy to come to them, as if we will someday be able to gain entrance through God's gates by standing at them and shouting: "Hey, no one called me. No one gave me directions. It's not my fault."

When I am in jails or juvenile centers, I confront this attitude all the time. If I hear someone tell me, "I'm bored," I am always very direct with my response: "You aren't bored, you're boring! It is not life's job to entertain you."

I can walk into any jail or any church and see two people sitting inches from each other. One is wrapped in the joy of Christ; one is wrapped in a cloak of boredom, even hostility. They are both in the same room, both in the same environment, both in the same circumstance, but one has found the ability to self-initiate joy and the other is waiting for someone to entertain him or her.

I often tell inmates that they can choose to be a "prisoner of the county" or, like the Apostle Paul, a "prisoner for Christ." It is similar to the two criminals whose crosses were only meters apart with Christ in between. One sees Christ through the eyes of hope and compassion; he finds both the Messiah and salvation. The other sees Christ through only the eyes of his own bitterness and blame. When he saw Jesus, he saw a criminal, just like him. One is blessed, the other cursed; which do we want to model and lead young people to find in their lives—even in their direst circumstances?

That is the emphasis in this book, leading young people (in fact, all people) to find a sustainable, self-initiating joy. We want those around us, like Kelly, to be able to love like Jesus loved—no matter what circumstances life throws at them.

Self-Initiated Joy: Becoming the Beloved Blessing

> Rejoice in the Lord always, again I will say, Rejoice. Let your gentleness be known to everyone. The Lord is near. Do not worry about anything, but in everything by prayer and supplication with thanksgiving let your requests be made known to God. And the peace of God, which surpasses all understanding, will guard your hearts and your minds in Christ Jesus.
>
> Finally, beloved, whatever is true, whatever is honorable, whatever is just, whatever is pure, whatever is pleasing, whatever is commendable, if there is any excellence and if there is anything worthy of praise, think about these things. Keep on doing the things you have learned and received and heard and seen in me, and the God of peace will be with you. (Philippians 4:4–9)

I might be able to rejoice like Paul on a good day, but could I rejoice like he did while under arrest and facing death? Could I take the worst tyranny of my era and use it to turn my life into a life that praises God? Paul goes on to say:

> Not that I am referring to being in need, for I have learned to be content with whatever I have. I know what it is to have little, and I know what it is to have plenty. In any and all circumstances I have learned the secret of being well-fed and of going hungry, of having plenty and of being in need. I can do all things through him who strengthens me. (Philippians 4:11–13)

This is the ultimate blessing—a rejoicing that is not based upon my immediate circumstances, but based instead upon a deep, inner strength, unshakeable by external influences. In short, we long for those around us to be blessed *[makarios]* and to be a blessing *[eulogeo],* and in the blessing be blessed. Isn't that the desire of our heart of hearts? Isn't that what we long for and value most for Kelly and, indeed, for every child of God?

2 Adolescent or Adult: Which One Am I?

Jesus said to her, "Everyone who drinks of this water will be thirsty again, but those who drink of the water that I will give them will never be thirsty. The water that I will give will become in them a spring of water gushing up to eternal life." (John 4:13–14)

Would You Love Me If You Knew Me?

In the story of Jesus and the Samaritan woman at the well, two possible reasons for the woman to have come to draw water at noon are as follows: (1) to avoid the "proper women" of her community; and (2) to look for strangers who might be passing through. In the woman's misshapen viewpoint of life, Jesus appeared to her to be just such a stranger; he was a foreigner on the road at the outskirts of town, lingering alone by the well. In her mind, he was another prospective lover who might leave a coin on the counter when he left. She had spent her life being used, and now she was "using back." It wasn't love, but it filled the gap.

How could she know that Jesus would meet her on a radically deeper level? that he would meet her on a level far deeper than the well from which she would pour his water?

She flirted with our Lord! She tried to banter with him, let him in—but only on her level and under her terms. It was the only form of love she understood, and, after all, you can't describe something you've never tasted. However, Jesus would have none of her teasing. "Go, call your husband and come back" (John 4:16), he said. We can be very sure no man had ever said that to her before.

She didn't come to the well seeking more brackish water; she really came to the well to quench a more relenting thirst—for approval, to be loved or valued—even if it was just enough attention to get by for the day. She would try to find temporary solace in her promiscuous offer to this stranger by Jacob's well. Instead, she found living water, eternal springs, streams in her desert (and deserted) life. She had drunk from brackish waters so often that she actually thought they were sweet. Then Jesus offered her the crystal clear, pure water of God's abundant love, and she knew instantly she would never thirst again.

Christine first joined a gang at twelve. She was "jumped in" by every male member of the gang after they had doped her up and she could barely stand in her drunken stupor. Now at fourteen and incarcerated (yet again) for solicitation, she can't understand what it is like to be really loved. She can't trust anyone who would love her. She has no concept of love at all except a love that involves being used. Christine needs living water, and her well is really dry.

Perhaps Jesus didn't know that the woman at the well would be coming that noon—or perhaps he did. However, he definitely knew what she truly thirsted for on the deepest level of her existence: a stream in a huge merciless wasteland. She needed acceptance without conditions, love without being used. She needed to hear the words of the beloved blessing: "You are my beloved child, in you I find such joy."

Not, "In your body, . . ." not, "In our passion, . . ." not, "In the moment, . . ." but, "In you I am well pleased."

It is the same thing that Christine cries out for . . . despite the fact that she might never be able to verbalize her despair. But who among us hasn't tried to drink at a brackish well? Who among us hasn't mistaken acceptance for love and approval for blessing? How many of us would recognize the difference, especially if we had never tasted it?

When the Samaritan woman drank from the living waters of Jesus Christ, she ran from house to house proclaiming: "Come and see a man who told me everything I have ever done!" (John 1:29).

It doesn't sound like something most of us would want the whole town to know. After all, who in that town didn't already know all the things she had ever done (and probably made up some extra tidbits in the telling)? But what was she truly saying? "He knows everything I have ever done . . . and he still loves me!"

Twenty years ago, a youth group in Beaumont, Texas, asked me to write a theme song for their convention. When I asked what their theme was, a voiced steeped in a Texas-sized drawl said, "Kiss a fuhrooog." When I figured out that they were asking me to write a theme song about frog kissing I said: "I am totally inexperienced in this area. Help me understand what that means to you."

Young people in that region sent me a number of letters talking about their theme. The song that I eventually wrote, "Would You Love Me If You Knew Me?" is really just a compilation of their precious thoughts.

> Would you love me if you knew me, what I really am inside? Through all this fear and doubting I try so hard to hide.

> Would you love me if you knew me, through these masks that I have on? If I really let you know me through this mask of being strong.

> I'd give my heart to you . . . if I could find it. I'd give my dream to you . . . but would you be kind to it?

> So until I really know that you're not going to turn away, I will wait until my heart knows you will stay.

> Would you love me if you knew me? I'm a silly, little child. And, I'd do most anything just for one approving smile.

> Would you love me if you knew me, just a frog who dreams of kings? But if you could only love me I could be most anything.

> I'd give my heart to you . . . if I could find it. I'd give my dream to you . . . but would you be kind to it?

> So until I really know that you're not going to turn away, I will wait until my heart knows you will stay.

Jesus really knows us and still loves us. That is the beloved blessing. That is the living water. As Paul said so well: "But God proves his love for us in that while we still were sinners Christ died for us" (Romans 5:8).

Isn't that amazing? Isn't that unfathomable? We are loved beyond the approval of this world. We are loved without having to try and earn the fickle acceptance of others. We confuse acceptance and approval with love and then work so hard to obtain a love that is already given. It is a love that is based not in what we do, not in what we have, but in our integrity, our dignity simply as children of a loving God.

Don't young people thirst for that kind of water? hunger for that kind of food? My heart aches for Christine to hear that message, taste that water. I long for her to know she is the woman at the well, she can quit drinking the brackish water of false acceptance and turn instead to the living well and the loving waters of Jesus Christ. "He knows everything that I ever have done and still loves me."

If we can't understand the difference between the brackish waters of approval and acceptance and the true love of Jesus Christ, how will we ever help the Christines of our world?

Adolescing and Adulthood

Christ's gift of belovedness inevitably leads to a new sense of maturity tied neither to chronological age or cultural roles. We are mature when we know we are beloved and that Christ wants us to bless others in the same way—beyond approval and beyond acceptance (unconditional blessing). Our definitions of *adolescing* and *adulthood* change in response to this knowledge. In this book, I define *adolescence* in these terms: "As long as my peers interpret my self-esteem, I am adolescing."

Alternatively I define *an adult* in this manner: "When I know my values and can make my life choices (including to whom I will be held accountable) based upon those values, I am an adult."

Our esteem of self and love of others lies purely in the dignity offered to us by a compassionate God. Neither our esteem nor the esteem of others is up for grabs—it is a given, a God-given. How could we respond with anything but love to such an offer? If we can embrace even a millionth of this beloved blessing, it gives us a profound humility toward life and a lucid vision to share: "Christine, he knows everything that we have ever done . . . and he still loves us."

It is easy to see—by these definitions—that we might be surrounded by, and perhaps included with, countless numbers of adolescing people who constantly walk about in adult bodies. So many of us are still trying to impress others, to gain their acceptance or approval through what we buy, wear, or do.

By our definition, adolescence is not a stage tied to pubescence, but instead, it is tied to our ability (or inability) to identify our values, create supportive friendships, and make core life choices based upon those values. In our culture many people's sense of belovedness fluctuates with the changing opinions of the culture or their peer groups. Their primary question for decision making is "What will others think?"

They make buying decisions and major life choices not based upon what they value, or even upon what they earn, but instead upon impressing others. Their sense of belovedness fluctuates with the "oohs" and "ahhs" of a new car, the comforts of a larger house, or the attractiveness of a new garment. Are they not just like Christine, only more subtle and culturally accepted in how they meet their needs? All the while they cry out with an inner emptiness that is overwhelming and that constantly gnaws away at their sense of worth.

The deep, encompassing thirst of the woman at the well, or even the confusion of Christine in her detention cell, will not be satiated by anything material or transient. Instead, such a hunger cries out for something much more profound; only something with substance and meaning can satisfy this emptiness.

What Do I Value? Why Am I Valued?

It is important to pause and reflect at this point and ask, "Have I made the effort to name what I value?" Or, more precisely, "Whom do I value?" Have each of us followed God's commands and written our values "on the doorposts of your houses and on the gates" (Deuteronomy 6:9)?

Can each of us clearly name whom we value and why *we* are valuable, and then set our course by the answers to those questions? Are our values so deeply engrained within us that they help set our agenda for each week? Where will we spend our limited resources of time, money, and emotional strength?

Here is a question I often ask myself as an accountability check: "If I hired a private detective to walk ten feet behind me for an entire week and told that person to check my appointment calendar, listen in on my conversations, and see where I pulled out my wallet, what—at the end of the week—would that detective tell me about my values?"

If what we do, where we go, who we hang with, and how we spend our resources does not match what we value, then we have to face the uncomfortable possibility that we are not just living inconsistently but that we ourselves are still adolescing.

Am I Still Adolescing?

I wonder if the Apostle Peter ever became frustrated with his constant failures. He wanted to walk on water, then sank miserably. He accurately named Christ as the Messiah, but, within a heartbeat, he was called Satan by the Lord himself. He wanted to build a tabernacle on Mount Tabor and was silenced by none other than God. He wanted to stand by Jesus in our Lord's darkest hours but then denied Jesus when he was questioned by a woman in the crowd. Peter received a personal commission from our Lord and was then castigated for questioning John's faith. He wanted to lead the Church to the Gentiles but ended up rebuked by Paul for backsliding.

However, mustn't we admit that at least Peter failed where no one else even dared to go? The disciples may have snickered when Peter sank into the waters of the Galilean lake, but they were laughing from the deck of the boat. None of them tried to step out that far on the waters of their faith. Peter might have denied Jesus, but at least he did so in the courtyard of the high priest. Would we have followed Jesus out that far?

I write this book not as an expert at faith but as a fellow traveler who wants to fail boldly if I am going to fail at all. I want to fail out that far. If I am going to be a fool, let me at least be "fools for the sake of Christ," as Paul would say (1 Corinthians 4:10). Peter fails, but he fails boldly. He becomes a fool, but he does so openly. Peter wants the world to know that he failed fearlessly but Jesus Christ, his Lord and friend, still loved him.

Peter is held accountable to his values by Jesus and then holds himself accountable to others so that he will never again deny Jesus. That is one of the most important aspects of faithful maturity: "Whom will I ask to hold me accountable—in word and deed—to my values?"

Change Them or Walk with Them

Many books about helping the Christines of our world do not begin with the most appropriate question: "Am I still adolescing?"

Instead, many books about reaching out to young people begin their focus by saying how to change them. Yet, most young people are doing the best they can in the values vacuum we have left them. We left them sitting at the Samaritan well. We pulled out of their lives and turned them over to be raised by programs and institutions. Institutions can hold their bodies but not their hearts.

In all of my outreach programs we say this: "If you have come here to change kids, to tell them what to do or convert them, then you are not going to fit comfortably into our ministry approach. However, if you have come here to journey with young people, if you are willing to ask the same questions of yourself that you are asking of them, then this is the right place for you."

We don't have to be "totally adult" to help those who are adolescing. But we at least need to be "adulting."

What Do You Seek?
(We Can't Send People Where We Won't Go)

I hope you have come to this book so you can make the hard, honest journey with the Christines of our world. I hope you have come here to walk the path to spiritual maturity with her and not tell her what to do. This was the gift Jesus offered his first two followers, John and Andrew (who were also probably in their teens when they met him).

> The next day John again was standing with two of his disciples, and as he watched Jesus walk by, he exclaimed, "Look, here is the Lamb of God!" The two disciples heard him say this, and they followed Jesus. When Jesus turned and saw them following, he said to them, "What are you looking for?" They said to him, "Rabbi" (which translated means Teacher), "where are you staying?" He said to them, "Come and see." They came and saw where he was staying, and they remained with him that day. (John 1:35–39)

Isn't that a compelling story? The first two statements of Jesus to his first two followers were "What are you looking for?" and "Come and see."

"What are you looking for?" also translates into "What do you desire?" "Where is your treasure?" "What do you value?"

The disciples' simple response, "Where do you live?" identifies for us the true desire of all seekers of God throughout the ages. They simply desired to be with Jesus. They wanted only to be in relationship with him. All they valued was to be with our Lord wherever he went. And, our beautiful Savior, consistent still to this day, gave them the greatest gift we could ever give to someone like Christine, he invites them to "Come and see."

"Come, live with me. Come, see where I spend my time, see what I value. Walk the path with me."

The early Christians were called followers of the Way. They walked the path with Jesus. When Jesus said "come and see," they literally "up and went."

This is the deepest longing of our young people today—not a new program or curriculum to tell them what to do or what they should value but caring, compassionate adults who will walk the path to wholeness with them. Let them be the hired detective who follows us around for a week. Let the young people examine where we spend our resources, let them tell us what we value by observing our lives.

Time! Jesus took time in the middle of feeding thousands, healing all known diseases, and completing all the prophecies of the Old Testament. Our Lord bent his life around two teenage followers who came out of the desert to follow him. What about Christine? What about those who are right around us? Jesus would walk with them, and he invites us to do the same.

"Please, Just Spend Time with Me"

What was the longest walk you ever took? I don't mean the longest distance, for long distances can seem like nothing when you are walking with the right person. I remember walks to tell young inmates that their father or mother had died. I remember walks to the court where an eighteen-year-old prisoner I was ministering to was sentenced to forty-three years. I remember walks up the front steps to tell a mother that her son had been arrested for murder. I remember walking to a gravesite with my brother when his young baby died.

In every situation I asked myself some version of the same question: "How do I make you feel valuable now?" "What do you need now?" "How can I love you best?" And I often hear some version of the same response that John and Andrew gave Jesus: "Where do you live?" Only it sounds like this: "Please, just spend time with me."

You have your walks too, don't you? Perhaps you are in the middle of one even as you read this. Even if you are not, we both know that life is filled with these walks, and they can devastate us when we walk them alone. Yet, we do not have to walk alone. Jesus can still take our longest walks and make them into the shortest moments. He proclaims, "I am!" "I am everywhere, all the time, wherever you need me—I am there."

I know that I can handle the difficulties I face as long as I take my daily walk with Jesus. I literally meet him where my driveway meets the street, and I can hear him say, "Here I am, Jerry, come and see." On days when I think I am too busy to walk, I can even feel his presence there asking, "Are you going to leave without me today?"

It is on those days that I never get ahead. My perspective is off, my thoughts aren't centered. If I have too many of those days in a row, I can't even tell which way is north anymore. I will boldly tell you that I am addicted to walking with Jesus. "My Jesus, where are you living today?"

"Come and See—Walk with Me"

When our Lord invited the disciples to "come and see," he was actually asking them to live with him, to travel with him and, indeed, he was asking them to become disciples. The custom for disciples in Christ's day was not just to listen to the master in a school or a synagogue for a one-hour-a-week lecture. They literally left everything to follow him, to see what the master did on a daily basis. They walked with the master wherever he went. Jesus spoke frequently about the walk, to his disciples:

> Jesus said to them, "The light is with you for a little longer. Walk while you have the light, so that the darkness may not overtake you. If you walk in the darkness, you do not know where you are going. While you have the light, believe in the light, so that you may become children of light." (John 12:35–36)

The term for *walk* in this particular verse is *peripateo,* literally meaning to "walk all around," which is related to the word *parapet,* the walkway that encircles a castle or a city's defensive wall. The first thing that Nehemiah, the biblical leader, did when he returned to the broken city of Jerusalem was to walk the parapet.

> I went out by night by the Valley Gate past the Dragon's Spring and to the Dung Gate, and I inspected the walls of Jerusalem that had been broken down and its gates that had been destroyed by fire. Then I went on to the Fountain Gate and to the King's Pool, but there was no place for the animal I was riding to continue. (Nehemiah 2:13–14)

To walk the parapet with Jesus has become one of my favorite images of prayer. Every day I try to spend some time with Jesus walking the parapet of both my family and my community, praying for and listening to where God would have me be available today, finding where the walls are broken and the streets need to be repaired.

> Your ancient ruins shall be rebuilt;
>   you shall raise up the foundations of many generations;
> you shall be called the repairer of the breach,
>   the restorer of streets to live in.
>
> (Isaiah 58:12)

Many times we say we value Jesus, but do we spend daily time walking with him? If he said, "Come and see," would we "up and go"? Do we walk the parapets with him, hunting out the breaches in our walls and the streets that need restoring in our lives? Do we walk to the Samaritan wells in our communities? Do we walk into Christine's cell with his cup of living water?

The Right Questions

When people come to me and ask to volunteer to work with troubled youth, I tell them that the essence of our ministry is as simple—and as difficult—as listening like Jesus listened, asking the questions that he would ask. It was the mark of Jesus's life that he would wait to speak until he could ask the right question at the right time to the right person or people. He asked his Apostles, "What are you looking for?" (John 1:38) and, "Who do you say that I am?" (Luke 9:20). He asked his followers, "What will it profit them if they gain the whole world but forfeit their life?" (Matthew 16:26). He asked the self-righteous religious rulers, "How can you speak good things, when you are evil?" (Matthew 12:34).

The blind called out for his mercy and Jesus responded with, "What do you want me to do for you?" They cried out for sight and Jesus opened their eyes. A man, crippled for forty-two years, laid by the pool of Bethsaida and Jesus asked, "Do you want to be well?"

I tell the high-risk young people I work with that asking the right question is a critical trait of healthy leadership. I tell our mentors, "When you can ask questions for a total of five minutes and help a young person talk for fifty-five, then you are ready to take over the program."

Jesus asked the right questions: "What do you seek?" "What do you value?"

Great leaders ask the right questions!

You will see an amazing thing if you visit the Ebenezer Baptist Church in Atlanta, Georgia. On the wall by the entrance are pictures of the pastors of the church. There's the Reverend Williams who married Jennie Parks. Their daughter, Alberta Christine Williams married a man named Martin Luther King Sr., who replaced Reverend Williams as pastor of the Church. Reverend and Mrs. King had a son name Martin Luther King Jr., who would take over the church from his father, and then there was Dr. Otis Moss who was followed by Dr. Joseph Lawrence Roberts Jr., who is the senior pastor today.

What a thought-provoking wall. When I saw it I asked myself: "Did Reverend Williams ever consider that his grandson would lead the greatest civil rights movement in the twentieth century? Did he have a clue when he dusted that boy off from a fall on the sidewalk or served him a helping of potatoes at a family dinner that his grandchild would someday challenge the value system of the most powerful nation on earth?"

It is highly unlikely that the grandfather had any such insights anymore than any grandfather has aspirations that his grandchild will be blessed. Yet, the modeling of both the parents and the grandparents led Dr. Martin Luther King Jr., to ask the right question of his nation and, indeed, our world. King asked us to dream about the world we wanted to leave our children, grandchildren, our loved ones, the next generation that would inherit the beloved blessing. What would we value for them? Do we want a nation of division, prejudice, and hatred, or do we have something greater in mind, a greater dream, a greater vision? Which will it be—division or the vision?

> I have a dream that one day this nation will rise up and live out the true meaning of its creed: "We hold these truths to be self-evident: that all men are created equal." I have a dream that one day on the red hills of Georgia the sons of former slaves and the sons of former slave-owners will be able to sit down together at a table of brotherhood. I have a dream that one day even the state of Mississippi, a desert state, sweltering with the heat of injustice and oppression, will be transformed into an oasis of freedom and justice. I have a dream that my four children will one day live in a nation where they will not be judged by the color of their skin but by the content of their character. I have a dream today.

> (Oates, *Let the Trumpet Sound,* pp. 254–255)

Dr. King was given a dream, a vision based upon the values of his parents and grandparents—and, indeed, the faith of the founders of the United States. He spoke openly about passing that dream on to his own four children. Will we speak about our values as openly and model them as transparently to Christine so that she too might have a dream?

> Then afterward
>   I will pour out my spirit on all flesh;
> your sons and your daughters shall prophesy,
>   your old men shall dream dreams,
>   and your young men shall see visions.

> (Joel 2:28)

The whole emphasis of the outreach programs I direct (both in churches and in detention centers) is helping young people dream dreams and see visions. Our programs help young people identify what they value and help them choose life-long friendships that will support them in developing those values. I never leave a session without asking them some variation of "Who could you love a little better this week?" You see, for these youth, Christ's water will ultimately be found, not in what we give them but in what they give to someone else.

Teens who know what they value are far less likely to be swayed by the pressure of a peer or today's media. They are the young people who understand the difference between true unconditional love and mere acceptance and approval. Such value-strengthened youth are resilient to negative pressure and can even be resilient to the abusiveness of their own adolescing parents. Many of these youth (who may have once been incarcerated or expelled) turn around and become servant leaders in our communities, shaping the lives of their peers and even changing the prejudicial attitudes that many communities have toward young people.

These are strong kids, resilient kids; they are no longer victims of their circumstances. They are blessed, and they are a blessing. The process of arming our young people with this kind of strength is not difficult, but it is deliberate, and it all begins with each of us asking them, "Whom do you value?" and offering them the only answer that will help them become compassionate adults: "Come and see how much I value you."

Where is the Samaritan well in your city? Have you drank at the well? Do you know the unconditional love of Jesus Christ? Where, in your town, is Christine sitting in a daze of confusion and pain? Are you willing to become living water to her—beyond acceptance and approval?

Where in your community would Jesus lead? Can you hear him turn to you and say, "Come and see"? Will you "up and go"?

3 The Four Habits of a Healthy Follower

Joy Is Practiced, Not Found

How can we model what we don't know? How can we preach a joy we don't experience or profess a love we have never embraced? Often a "Grand Canyon" exists between our profession of faith and our practice of love because . . . well, we don't practice love, we leave it to chance. If we feel like it, then maybe we will offer it. Yet, love wasn't an option to Jesus, it was a commandment.

> I give you a new commandment, that you love one another. Just as I have loved you, you also should love one another. By this everyone will know that you are my disciples, if you have love for one another. (John 13:34–35)

Why do we make a habit of so many mundane things and yet leave our faith life—our love life with God and God's people—to chance? All too often we pray only when we feel like it or when we are troubled. We read the Scriptures when we are looking for a quote or seeking solace from some trial. We pray with others when someone is in trouble or when challenges in life have invaded our comfort zone. We are like an athlete who wants to go to the Olympics, but we only want to practice when we feel like it. We are like the father who says, "I need to spend more time with my family" but then never actually schedules time with them.

I remember being stunned to hear the piercing speech of a friend of mine who recently retired as the chief executive officer of a large, regional trust company: "Many of you here want my job. However, I need to tell you. I just returned from my youngest daughter's wedding, and I didn't even know her maid of honor's name. If you want to live a life where, at retirement, you can't even recognize your children's best friends, then you are welcome to this position."

Do we have any intimate friends? any friends that know us well enough to hold us accountable to our values? Are our friendships really just peers from work or have we learned to combine our values and our friendships to strengthen our families, our communities, our faith?

Paul tells us that our faith is too important to be left to emotions or chance, or to be fit into our schedule after all the other tasks and to-dos have been accomplished:

> Do you not know that in a race the runners all compete, but only one receives the prize? Run in such a way that you may win it. Athletes exercise self-control in all things, they do it to receive a perishable wreath, but we an imperishable one. So I do not run aimlessly, nor do I box as though beating the air, but I punish my body and enslave it, so that after proclaiming to others I myself should not be disqualified. (1 Corinthians 9:24–27)

Living a faithful life is the hardest race; it cannot be left to coincidence or emotions. We are raised in a culture that sees ethics and values as an end and not as a means. So we manipulate the means thinking we can recover our faith in the end. How long does it take for us to learn that if we don't control the means, we cannot control the end?

> Then he told them a parable: "The land of a rich man produced abundantly. And he thought to himself, 'What should I do, for I have no place to store my crops?' Then he said, 'I will do this: I will pull down my barns and build larger ones, and there I will store all my grain and my goods. And I will say to my soul, Soul, you have ample goods laid up for many years, relax, eat, drink, be merry.' But God said to him, 'You fool! This very night your life is being demanded of you. And the things you have prepared, whose will they be?' So it is with those who store up treasures for themselves but are not rich toward God." (Luke 12:16–21)

It is not just an issue of dying before we are able to recover our ends. It is not just an issue of eternal importance; it is also an issue of immediate importance. When we do not practice our faith daily and set aside time for our Lord, we miss so much joy in the present! It is the delight of God to give us joy and to be in relationship with us on an intimate, moment-to-moment basis.

I have met so many guards in prisons that say, "Don't rock my boat, I only have seventeen years until I retire, and I don't want any hassles." Seventeen years is 6,209 days (if you include leap years)—6,209 days of drudgery. Yet, what makes us think that if our lives are filled with drudgery now, we will have the sudden ability to experience unparalleled joy 6,209 days from now? Our Lord wants to offer us today joy—not just someday joy. God has immediate and eternal joy in store for us. God wants all our days to be glad.

> Satisfy us in the morning with your steadfast love,
>   so that we may rejoice and be glad all our days.
>
> (Psalm 90:14)

This type of joy is practiced—not found—and the Lord desires to fill our lives with this joy on this very day. This type of joy cannot be left to chance and isn't an innate part of our character. It is a choice (a *eulogeo* or a blessing) that we make to commit ourselves to the Lord's way. We need to practice our faith. We need to work at it now not because—like the fool and his grain houses—we could die tomorrow, but because of the joy we will miss today if we don't wake up and breathe in the Holy Spirit.

The Practice of Faith

Reclaiming Lives

In prison and juvenile outreach programs, I have a very short period of time to help young people reconstruct their lives before they go back onto the streets. Most restoration programs focus on new techniques—communication skills, anger management, addiction awareness—never realizing that these are just the symptoms, not the disease. Though techniques are important, they are only 5 percent of the cure. We will explore this idea later, but here's the rub: Incarcerated people don't *want* to come back to jail, but they do *expect* to come back to jail. Changing techniques can change symptoms, but the disease has to be treated on a deeper level. The premiere agent of change is the *desire* to change, not the *techniques* of change.

How many of us have no expectation of joy or a mistaken belief that joy can only come from an external—not an internal and an eternal—source? How many of us have thumbed through the latest how-to craze only to find it was a fad? How many of us now thumb our noses at all new fads because our expectation is that they will just be another short-term, temporary, quick-fix program focusing on techniques that we cannot sustain beyond the initial excitement?

Joy is not a quick fix. It is not a technique. It is a way of life, a compilation of habits that, when practiced, will sustain us on our journey of faith. The psalmist puts it like this:

> Trust in the LORD, and do good;
> so you will live in the land, and enjoy security.
> Take delight in the LORD,
> and he will give you the desires of your heart.
>
> Commit your way to the LORD;
> trust in him, and he will act.
> He will make your vindication shine like the light,
> and the justice of your cause like the noonday.
>
> (Psalm 37:3–6)

Trust, delight, and commit—that is our part. These are not beliefs to stumble upon. They are character traits to be developed, with specific ways to develop them. However, it takes an immense amount of *trust* and *commitment*—words our society does not like at all today—on our part to find this kind of delight. We have to commit to trust in a world of sarcastic doubt. We have to choose to delight in a time where cynics seem wise. We don't come by these qualities naturally.

In building habits, the first ninety days are always the most critical. That is when most people quit because the habits feel unnatural and one must constantly remind oneself to act differently. Many fail once or twice and then give up saying, "See, I will never be able to change." Unfortunately, a long list of people usually are only too willing to agree with them.

Yet, just around ninety days, subtle, internal changes begin to occur for those who persist. One begins to desire the practiced behavior, even to set one's calendar by it.

It is similar with the habits of faith. Your body begins to crave waking a little earlier to read the Scriptures. You look forward to time with valuable and faithful friends to discuss your relationship with God and one another. You hunger for prayer and God's whisper in your ear.

In my own efforts to help young men and women seek a mature faith life, I tell them about four critical habits they need to practice to "make it on the outs" (outside the prison walls). I like to remind young people that Paul was also a prisoner, but he never called himself a "prisoner of Rome." He was always a "prisoner in the Lord" (Ephesians 3:1, 4:1; Colossians 4:10; and 2 Timothy 1:8). Can you see the subtle yet critical difference? Paul believed that Christ was greater than any circumstance, and he could use all circumstances toward God's glory. These young people need to know they can either be a prisoner of the county or a prisoner in the Lord, but only they can make that choice.

Once they become prisoners in the Lord, everything that happens to them in jail points toward God. Their incarceration can actually become the greatest university in their lives if they use it to draw nearer to God. It is the perfect opportunity, I tell them, to start practicing the habits of faith that will help them "make it on the outs."

The Four Critical Habits

Habit One: Walk with Jesus

The first habit, as you might suspect, is to daily walk the parapet of your life with Jesus. Paul called it "pray without ceasing" (1 Thessalonians 5:17). Brother Lawrence, the seventeenth-century monk who, amid humbly washing dishes for his brothers, counseled bishops, kings, and popes with his letters, called it "practicing the presence of God." After a lifetime of listening to what others tell us is important and paying heed to the voices of this world, it is hard for us to turn off those false messages of acceptance and approval and instead tune in to the often countercultural messages of Jesus.

Before I understood that God is more likely to compel us than speak to us, I would often be oblivious to God's call. I could not hear God because I was using only one of my many senses. I can remember sessions at the dinner table when I would ask each one of my family members, "What did God say to you today?" Then, one day—after realizing how difficult a time my wife and children were having with that question—I asked myself, "How often does God actually speak to me verbally?"

I began to realize that God most often communicates with me through a stirring of the soul, but I wasn't attributing those moments to God. Someone or something would randomly come to my mind, or I would feel like I needed to stop in at a rest home or jail. When I paid attention to that prompting, I would often find myself stopping in during a critical moment of a person's life.

Soon I began to change my family dinner question to "How did you experience God today?" It may seem subtle, but I went from getting blank stares and somewhat forced answers from my family members to creating an opening for a whole different type of communication: "I felt God's touch in the warmth of the sun on my face this morning." "I felt God in grandma's hug." "I really felt like I needed to call my friend Sharon today and she said that she 'just hoped she could talk to someone.' God's timing was perfect." And, of course, there was always, "I heard God telling me you should raise my allowance."

To walk with God is to go through each day completely receptive to God's presence. After all, God gave us all of our senses, so God would undoubtedly delight in our using each one of them to reach us.

Habit Two: Study God's Word

The richest moments in your day could well be the moments before dawn when you can—without distraction—greet the Lord in prayer and the Scriptures. In that quiet time, before the rush of day is upon us, we can align ourselves with the only one who can offer us the beloved blessing of a full-and-filled (fulfilled) life.

The word is rich, and between its pages are eternal answers to every situation known on earth. Paul says it like this:

Proclaim the message; be persistent whether the time is favorable or unfavorable, convince, rebuke, and encourage, with the utmost patience in teaching. (2 Timothy 4:2)

Above all, demand the most from your Bible—not just to become more learned—but to become more compassionate. The Pharisees studied the Scriptures to become more learned, but they lacked compassion.

The Scriptures should be read with a bias for compassion—not to become more judgmental or scholarly than others—but read with a bias to become more humble and increasingly gracious. The heart of the Scriptures may well be found in this statement of Micah:

> He has told you, O mortal, what is good;
>   and what does the LORD require of you
> but to do justice, and to love kindness,
>   and to walk humbly with your God?
>
> (Micah 6:8)

Lay the word of God open before you and pray, "Holy Spirit, use this word to make me more compassionate, help me to be kinder—especially to those who receive no kindness—and teach me to be humbler each day."

Reread the words of John 3:16—just the first four: "For God so loved . . ."

Here is the bias of God. God so loved us that God acted . . . and the action was to give us Jesus as a sacrifice for our sin. The bias of God is love. Look at how the Apostle John put it:

> Beloved, let us love one another, because love is from God, everyone who loves is born of God and knows God. Whoever does not love does not know God, for God is love. (1 John 4:7–8)

Could we not spend the rest of our lives just contemplating that Scripture passage? Wouldn't it be better to fully incorporate that Scripture passage into our hearts than to know all the verses in the Bible and yet not understand compassion?

Let yourself be completely enveloped by the incredible compassion of God and his Son, Jesus. When you study God's word, examine it with an intentional bias for compassion, for our God has a bias for mercy that you will see continually displayed—especially in his Son.

Let the Scriptures guide your way, not for the sake of becoming more intelligent or judgmental, but for the distinct purpose of becoming more compassionate. The psalmist sings out: "Your word is a lamp to my feet and a light to my path" (Psalm 119:105).

Give this light to the young people around you. If they see that your path is lit by the lamp of God's word, they will also seek to carry that treasure into the darkest times of their lives. They will acquire the eternal gift that is good for all seasons. Give the young people around you a thirst for God's word that will become the bookends of their lives and the triangulating star of their destiny. Give them a bearing that will far outlast our days on earth. Give them God's word.

Do not delay. Tomorrow morning set your clock at least a half-hour earlier. Don't use that time to read more in the newspaper or watch another half-hour of morning shows. Instead, use that time with the intentional purpose of looking up the words *love, compassion,* and *mercy* in the concordance of your Bible. Follow those references to their sources in the Old and New Testaments. Remember to pray as you read, "Holy Spirit, show me how to be more compassionate and humble today."

Habit Three: Participate Fully in a Same-Gender Accountability Group

Among Paul's earliest writings were his letters to the Thessalonians. In them, he compels young people to encourage each other but also to admonish the unruly:

> Therefore encourage one another and build up each other, as indeed you are doing.
>
> But we appeal to you, brothers and sisters, to respect those who labor among you, and have charge of you in the Lord and admonish you, esteem them very highly in love because of their work. Be at peace among yourselves. And we urge you, beloved, to admonish the idlers, encourage the fainthearted, help the weak, be patient with all of them. See that none of you repays evil for evil, but always seek to do good to one another and to all. Rejoice always, pray without ceasing, give thanks in all circumstances, for this is the will of God in Christ Jesus for you. (1 Thessalonians 5:11–18)

These words express to the Thessalonians (largely a Gentile church) how to keep strong in their faith. The same is true for us today. In a culture of "pagan" values; of self-righteous, religious purists; and a materialization of the Gospel, we desperately need to be with other believers who are encouraging, helping, rejoicing, who pray without ceasing, and even admonish one another.

To put *admonish* in a sentence with *encourage, help, rejoice,* and *pray* seems odd. It is but one-fifth of the characteristics with which Paul charges the fledgling church, and admonishment without the other four traits is simply criticism. However, the word is in there, and the word *admonishment* should be a part of our lives too. The term *admonishment* means "to warn gently," "to caution," or "to put in mind." It *doesn't* mean "to tear down," "destroy," or "criticize." Criticism is something we do to fulfill our own self-rationalized anger (and most anger is self-rationalized). However, admonishment has a singular purpose: to speak the truth with grace.

Here is the rub. We are being called upon by Paul as members of the Body of Christ to seek people with whom we can share the tasks of encouraging, helping, rejoicing, praying, and admonishing. We could offer just the first four tasks of community and be pleasant with one another, but that would never move our relationship beyond platitudes. Jesus wants us to move beyond the plastic wrapping and into the depths of accountable community.

Think of accountability (seeking out people who will hold us to our values even if they have to admonish us) as developing a personal "carbon copy" or "cc" list, those whom we will "cc" about the trials, actions, and choices in our lives. In Paul's letter to Philemon, he "carbon copies" others who will hold Philemon accountable.

That "cc" list apparently includes Philemon's wife and son. It also includes Timothy, the highly regarded young "student" of Paul; and Archippus, one of the most beloved elders of the Thessalonica church. Paul then goes on to include the entire church that meets at Philemon's house.

In the face of a "cc" list like that, it would be hard not to make the right choices. Similarly, in our lives we need to build a "cc" list or an accountability group that will keep us responsible for asking the right questions and making the right choices. We need to allow these people to encourage our strengths and discourage our weaknesses. Seeking people who will hold us accountable to our values is, as we have said, one of the most critical steps we can take toward spiritual maturity.

Who is on your personal "cc" list? Who will help you discern between good and evil? Have you intentionally picked people who will hold you accountable to your values whether you feel like it or not? Are they holding you to values that align with the compassion of the Scriptures? We need to seek those people and, in turn, teach that quality to the youth whom we serve. We need to model to young people a life that seeks values over approval and not be afraid of being corrected when we are on the wrong course.

Seek others who will encourage, help, rejoice, pray always, and admonish you. They will tell you the truth with grace, the only truth that will set you free.

> Then Jesus said to the Jews who had believed in him, "If you continue in my word, you are truly my disciples; and you will know the truth, and the truth will make you free." (John 8:31–32)

These are relationships beyond platitudes, beyond our "Sunday best"; these are relationships that even welcome admonishment! These are the intimate kind of friendships that last not a lifetime, but an eternity.

Do not leave relationships like this to chance. That is perhaps the most important lesson we can also pass on to the young people around us. These are not circumstantial friendships. These are friendships you seek to foster and purposely develop toward a singular end, and that's not easy in a culture that prefers platitudes and pleasantries. To have that depth of friendship involves meeting regularly, refusing to go back to platitudes, and knowing someone well enough to not accept, "I'm okay," as an answer to the question, "How are you?" These types of friendships ask, "How are you . . . really?"

Habit Four: Go Where Jesus Would Go

A few years ago, some bracelets and T-shirts swept the nation with the simple initials WWJD on them, meaning "What Would Jesus Do?" It was a very simple thing to remember and it impacted a lot of people who made that question a part of their daily lives. Yet, the question by itself is incomplete.

The complete question is not only "What would Jesus do?" but "Where would Jesus be?" Consider what Jesus risked when he went to heal his friend Lazarus. He was venturing within five miles of Jerusalem, where he was a wanted man. The disciples knew this; in fact Thomas says, "Let us also go, that we may die with him" (John

11:16). At great personal risk, Jesus went to embrace the broken family of a close friend.

Jesus went to visit the powerless—even when it put him (and his followers) at great personal risk. He reached out to Lazarus within miles of the High Priests who were actively seeking ways to have our Lord killed.

Can we possibly understand that Jesus would do the very same thing for us? He would come within death's grasp to deliver us from death. How do we know? Because that is what he did!

To ask, "What would Jesus do?" without asking, "Where would Jesus be?" is incomplete. To complete our faith, we must ask; "Where would Jesus be . . . in my community? Where is Lazarus's tomb in my town? Where, in my sphere of influence, are there people who are confused, frightened, broken, and even at the point of death?" That is where Jesus would be. That is where we must go. Once we go there, then the question, "What would Jesus do?" makes infinitely more sense.

To follow Jesus, to "come and see," to "walk the parapet" is to go where Jesus would go before we even ask, "What would Jesus do?" That beloved blessing of the God for his Son was not based upon what our Lord did, it was based upon where our Lord went. Jesus went into the Jordan to become available to God. Then he went into the desert to be sharpened and tried by Satan. Then he went directly into service "to bring good news to the poor" (Luke 4:18). The blessing was based upon how he made himself available to God's prompting even when it meant going to Jerusalem to die.

Where would the Messiah be in your community? Where are the empty wells? Where would you find the most abused people drinking from the most brackish water? Where do people go in your community to die of loneliness and rejection? Who are the most hated sinners near your home?

We are called to be light—but in the darkness. We are called to be streams—but in the desert. All too often I feel like I am little more than a candle in the closet. All too often the faithful of a church seem to be no more than lightbulbs in a chandelier factory. We shine among the shining. But will I go where Jesus would go and, in those places, ask, "What would Jesus do?"

Nothing makes my faith more concrete and visible to those I am called to lead than when I go to be among the "least of these" and even more so, when I take others with me. How do we learn compassion except by being compassionate?

When I look at my date book, is it filled with more than just the people who can "do something for me"? Are there people in my week who cannot give anything back to me except a hug or a smile? Are there forgotten people in our calendars? Do those people—the poor—call us "good news"? Do we visit the "tombs" in our hometown and ask "What would Jesus do . . . here?" What is the will of the Lord?

> He has told you, O mortal, what is good;
>   and what does the Lord require of you
> but to do justice, and to love kindness,
>   and to walk humbly with your God?
>
> (Micah 6:8)

I love the way Micah begins that sentence: "He has told you, O mortal." It means, "You already know what is good." We already know this stuff. We already know we can't practice what Jesus preached if we don't go where Jesus would go.

Compassion is not an option to the follower of Christ. To be a follower means to follow him where he would go. Compassion is not an option.

Could each of us hand our date book to an admonishing friend and say, "Find Jesus in there"—the Jesus at the tomb, the Jesus with the tax collectors, the Jesus waiting for the disreputable to come to the well.

The greatest promises of the Old Testament are for those who do justice, love mercy, and walk humbly with their God. We are told that when we move from blaming and pointing fingers to service, God will do an incredible work in our lives.

Love, compassion, service—all of this is "Going Where Jesus Would Go to Do What Jesus Would Do." It just doesn't fit nicely on one side of a medium T-shirt: GWJWGTDWJWD.

Enthusiasm Versus Burnout

We've all heard that enthusiasm is caught, not taught. This adage seems to be in direct contrast to the term *burnout,* which is so prevalent in our culture. However, burnout doesn't come from working too hard. It comes from working too hard without a purpose. We burn out when we can't figure out why we exist from one day to the next, or when we feel powerless to affect change in the chaos of our lives.

Jesus steps into our burnout and sets our hearts on fire. He gives us the new commandment. "Love one another. Just as I have loved you, you also should love one another" (John 13:34). It's like saying to the Samaritan woman, "Hey, you were a sinner when I loved you—now go love other sinners . . . and, the worse the sinner, the greater your compassion will mean to them."

Jesus gives us this charge, but he also tells us about the joy of living in such an open and forgiving way:

> Give, and it will be given to you. A good measure, pressed down, shaken together, running over, will be put into your lap, for the measure you give will be the measure you get back. (Luke 6:38)

We are supposed to be that place of safety and rest, that lap to others, especially the young.

Our Lord does not make it difficult; instead, God gives us a *yoke* that is easy (a term that means well-fit—it won't give us blisters while we work). Our commission is attainable. We are not called to change the world—we are called to change *our* world. Will the fire of your enthusiasm be enough to light the flame—not for another generation but for the generation that is sitting in your living room?

We cannot sustain that type of life-changing enthusiasm with a happenstance approach to faith. It takes discipline—habits practiced consistently and constantly.

4 Consistent Love Despite Inconsistent Behavior

So if anyone is in Christ, there is a new creation: everything old has passed away, see, everything has become new! (2 Corinthians 5:17)

A new heart I will give you, and a new spirit I will put within you, and I will remove from your body the heart of stone and give you a heart of flesh. (Ezekiel 36:26)

God's Viewpoint Versus Satan's Viewpoint

A New Thing

In the Hebrew language, *new* or *chadash* means "a fresh beginning"; it also means "renewed, rebuilt, and repaired." God desires to give us a fresh beginning, to make us new and renewed at the same time. God not only wants to give us a new name but a new heart as well. God wants to renew our vigor and compassion. God wants a renewed church and a restored people.

What is it that renews lives, families, churches, and even cities? Repeatedly, I have seen that purpose, vision, and a focus that is outward on compassion are the qualities that restore both a person and a people.

Perhaps the greatest story of restoration and renewal regarding the redemptive character of God is the Old Testament story of Hosea and his wayward wife Gomer. Hosea was a great prophet of God, and Gomer was a harlot. Yet, God told this holy prophet, Hosea, to marry Gomer as a symbol of our Lord's faithfulness to God's unfaithful people. Can you imagine Hosea's indignation at this request? He was a righteous, religious man, holy in God's eyes. She was an adulteress, a sinner worthy of being stoned by Jewish law. Though she sinned again and again, God would instruct Hosea to bring her back from her lovers' beds and even to buy her back when she had been sold into slavery.

In the sixth chapter, the story comes together and we see both the heart of God and a prophecy about Jesus:

> "Come, let us return to the LORD;
>> for it is he who has torn, and he will heal us;
>> he has struck down, and he will bind us up.
> After two days he will revive us;
>> on the third day he will raise us up,
>> that we may live before him.
> Let us know, let us press on to know the LORD;
>> his appearing is as sure as the dawn;
> he will come to us like the showers,
>> like the spring rains that water the earth."
>
> (Hosea 6:1–3)

It is God who wants to rename us—to restore us to, and give us a life of, unity and joy. God wants to bandage our wounds, revive us, raise us up that we may live a new life and hear our new name, our true name. If only we could embrace this promise and then offer it to the young people in our lives. Then the world would be renewed before our eyes!

Yet, there is one who does not want us to know this great news. One whose very name means "diabolical." One who has no desire for us to be renewed, restored, or renamed. It is he of whom Christ tells us to be wary: "Do not fear those who kill the body but cannot kill the soul, rather fear him who can destroy both soul and body in hell" (Matthew 10:28).

The Deceiver and His Tired Old Names

In my work with gang-involved youth, I have often run into the men who really direct the gangs. They are usually men in their forties or fifties who do not do any of the dirty work. Rather they get their youngest kids to sell their drugs and run their errands while the older gang members do their fighting or enforcement work.

Behind such a ringleader lays a string of used carcasses he has left behind when they no longer serve his dark purposes. He doesn't want to develop a relationship with his new recruits; he doesn't even care about their names (except as tools). He doesn't want to grow closer to them or understand their needs. He wants his own needs met, and these new recruits are merely toys and tools on his path to self-fulfillment.

If you want to know Satan, analyze the behavior of these men. Satan's minions reflect him in that the Prince of Darkness does not want a relationship with us. He doesn't want to know our names, our dreams, or our hopes—unless knowing these things will serve him. He has but one purpose: to hurt God by causing us to fall away from God's love.

Satan doesn't even hurt us to enjoy our pain. His only pleasure comes from watching God wince at our distress. He sucks us dry like a spider does to its victim, and all that time, Satan is not even looking in our eyes, but he is gawking into God's eyes and slobbering, "Does this hurt?"

In my biblical studies, I once did a lengthy study on the names of the Holy Spirit and the names of the Holy Spirit's nemesis. In that study, the names of Satan could be summed up in the word *KataDiabolos,* the literal translation of which would be, "Cast to the dung heap to rise from the dung heap."

When I was a kid, my father brought home a dingo (a wild breed of dog from Australia) that we could never train. One of the dingo's worst traits (besides chewing on his master's children) was his irrepressible desire to smell ghastly. It turns out that wild dogs don't like the aroma of their own bouquet. They actually think it is enticing to the opposite sex to reek like the dung or the carcass of another animal. We could forget about bathing this canine swine, first of all, because we wouldn't have the same number of digits when we were done with the bath as when we started, and second, because as soon as he was able to get outside of our reach, he would sniff out the nearest stench and roll in it again. Our dingo was never picky about how he smelled—as long as he smelled intolerable.

That is an apt description of Satan: The Accuser, the Deceiver, Satan, wants to coat us with the sins of our past (the dung heap) and say, "That's who you are—that's who you will always be."

Yet, Satan's ruse is a deception; it is a lie. Satan is the King of Half-Lies—but can there ever be anything such as a half-truth? Isn't a half-truth a whole lie? For example, Satan is right—we are sinners. It is true that we are unworthy of God's love. It is true that we have failed God and God's people by both omission and commission. But listen to the whole truth:

> When the Pharisees saw this, they said to his disciples, "Why does your teacher eat with tax collectors and sinners?" But when he heard this, he said, "Those who are well have no need of a physician, but those who are sick. Go and learn what this means, 'I desire mercy, not sacrifice.' For I have come to call not the righteous but sinners." (Matthew 9:11–13)

And . . .

> And hope does not disappoint us, because God's love has been poured into our hearts through the Holy Spirit that has been given to us.
>
> For while we were still weak, at the right time Christ died for the ungodly. Indeed, rarely will anyone die for a righteous person — though perhaps for a good person someone might actually dare to die. But God proves his love for us in that while we still were sinners Christ died for us. (Romans 5:5–9)

Sadly, sorrowfully, Satan is so much easier to believe than God. It is easier to roll around in the sins of our past and to call that our character than it is to embrace the unfathomable love of God and God's whole truth that we are loved individually and purposefully. But, it is also only when we have truly embraced the Whole Truth that we can become light and living water to others. That is when we become the beloved blessing.

Until that point we can only offer a half-truth love at best—a love with conditions. A love that is really more about acceptance and approval than about laying down our lives for others.

God's view of us is completely the opposite of Satan's. God loves us without conditions. I spend a lot of time sharing with mentors and youth about unconditionals: unconditional love, unconditional acceptance, and unconditional consistency. What is amazing about God's love is that God is most consistent when we are least consistent. Look again at the story of Gomer and Hosea. Examine the entire history of the Israelite people or read again our Lord's continual forgiveness of Peter; Jesus's consistent outreach to Thomas; his undying love of sinners, tax collectors, and prostitutes. When we were least consistent, Jesus was most consistent. When we were least acceptable, Jesus was most accepting. When we were least lovable, Jesus was most loving. Does that sound like the forgiveness we embrace for ourselves or the blessing we give to others? Look at the full truth of how Jesus responds to our sinfulness:

> Jesus, knowing that the Father had given all things into his hands, and that he had come from God and was going to God, got up from the table, took off his outer robe, and tied a towel around himself. Then he poured water into a basin and began to wash the disciples' feet and to wipe them with the towel that was tied around him. He came to Simon Peter, who said to him, "Lord, are you going to wash my feet?" Jesus answered, "You do not know now what I am doing, but later you will understand." Peter said to him, "You will never wash my feet." Jesus answered, "Unless I wash you, you have no share with me." Simon Peter said to him, "Lord, not my feet only but also my hands and my head!" Jesus said to him, "One who has bathed does not need to wash, except for the feet, but is entirely clean. And you are clean, though not all of you." For he knew who was to betray him, for this reason he said, "Not all of you are clean." (John 13:3–11)

Don't we want to be washed clean by our Servant-Prince? If you stopped right now—just for a moment—could you possibly feel God's tender hands healing your wounds, blessing you, restoring your God-given name of beloved? God is so desirous to give us our true name and to restore us to our true dignity. God's living water is unconditional love, acceptance, and consistency.

It is when we have been blessed by God's love that we can become the beloved blessing to the young people of our communities. Look at how Christ continues his commission at the Last Supper: "So if I, your Lord and Teacher, have washed your feet, you also ought to wash one another's feet" (John 13:14).

One of the first three questions I always ask young people at juvenile centers is, "How do you like to be treated?" Can you guess what they tell me?

"With respect . . ."

So I ask them, "How can I best show you my respect?" I am no longer surprised when their number one answer is simply, "Show up when you say you will."

To love like we are commanded—like Christ loved us—is to show up at the most important time in a young person's life, and there is no more important time to show up than when that young person is acting conditionally. We show our love when we stick with young people—especially when they act like they don't care anymore or even if they try to undermine the relationship. We may not agree with their behavior, and we are called to be upfront or to admonish when we don't agree with their behavior, but we still show up. Jesus's acceptance or approval has no conditions. No proviso to his blessing (that is the vocation of the Accuser). Which love have you embraced? Which love do you offer? Would you let him wash your feet without conditions? Will you wash the feet of others without provision? Those questions are at the heart of becoming a beloved blessing.

Conditional Love = Easily Manipulated People

No! It seems like a fairly easy word to say, yet how many of us can't get that word out of our mouths, finding ourselves the victims of other people's priorities and, as a result, unable to pursue our own purposes? The inability to say no is mirrored by the desire to seek approval. And the more our approval is tied to conditional statements the harder it is for us to say no. Sadly, the harder it is for us to say no to others, the easier we are to manipulate. Can you see why the words and the timing of the beloved blessing are so important? Those words were unconditional; they were attached to Jesus's availability to God not his accomplishments. The blessing was absolute, complete, and perfect in focus: "This is my Son, the Beloved, with whom I am well pleased" (Matthew 3:17).

If a person has known only conditional acceptance throughout his or her life then that person is very easy to manipulate. That person is like a target for people who are manipulators. Victims of conditional acceptance believe the following:

- "I just have to do more to be loved."
- "I just have to do what you want to be accepted."
- "I am loved because of what I do or have, not because of who I am."

In this world, some people are especially attuned to those who are famished for acceptance. They seem to have radar that is tuned into the vulnerable, and they have no problem taking advantage of those who are desperately seeking approval. Like a shark riding the currents from the deep ocean, manipulators seem able to smell when someone is hurting, they know when a child or adolescing person will do anything for acceptance, and they have a feeding frenzy on the wounded.

It is critical that we know that such deceivers exist in our world, and it is critical that we know and teach young people the traits of these deceivers and their addictive relationships—relationships that are built upon, "I will love you if . . ."

How the Deceiver Still Deceives

Imagine sitting around the campfire with Jesus one night after a long day of hiking. It is just Jesus, a small group of his disciples, and you. Somewhere in the conversation, one of those at the fire (maybe even you) asks Jesus to talk about temptation. In the glow of the fire, Jesus shares one of the most intimate stories in the whole Bible. A story about a battle between Satan and our Lord. A battle that is not just for our Lord's soul but, indeed, the soul of the very universe. This story could come from only Jesus himself, as he alone witnessed the whole event. Join him around the campfire two thousand years ago.

> Then Jesus was led up by the Spirit into the wilderness to be tempted by the devil. He fasted forty days and forty nights, and afterwards he was famished. The tempter came and said to him, "If you are the Son of God, command these stones to become loaves of bread." But he answered, "It is written,
> 'One does not live by bread alone,
>   but by every word that comes from the mouth of God.'"
> Then the devil took him to the holy city and placed him on the pinnacle of the temple, saying to him, "If you are the Son of God, throw yourself down, for it is written,
> 'He will command his angels concerning you,'
>   and 'On their hands they will bear you up,
> so that you will not dash your foot against a stone.'"
> Jesus said to him, "Again it is written, 'Do not put the Lord your God to the test.'"

> Again, the devil took him to a very high mountain and showed him all the kingdoms of the world and their splendor, and he said to him, "All these I will give you, if you will fall down and worship me." Jesus said to him, "Away with you, Satan! for it is written,
>> 'Worship the Lord your God,
>>> and serve only him.'"
>
> Then the devil left him, and suddenly angels came and waited on him.
>
> (Matthew 4:1–11)

This story takes place immediately after the beloved blessing. Jesus steps into the Jordan to become available to God and then instantaneously he is led about by the Spirit into the wilderness of Gehenna. Satan lets Jesus linger in the desert for forty days without food before he makes his move. It is a characteristic of Satan to wait for the opportune time, when we are most hungry, most thirsty, and most isolated.

When Satan approaches Jesus, he does so with three temptations: comfort, acceptance, and power or manipulation. Satan says, "If you are the Son of God, command these stones to become loaves of bread" (Matthew 4:3).

This is the first temptation, and each one gets progressively harder to resist. However, Satan usually has most of us trapped with this first barrage. It is the temptation to meet our physical needs or even just our need to stay within the safety of our own comfort zones. Satan is not just offering us bread (through the temptation of Jesus); he is offering to meet our physical and sensual needs, our need for immediate gratification. Satan also appeals to our desire for the illusion of safety and security—two things that Christ never promises us in this life.

> If you are the Son of God, throw yourself down, for it is written, "He will command his angels charge concerning you";
>> and "On their hands they will bear you up,
>
> so that you will not dash your foot against a stone."
>
> (Matthew 4:5)

When Satan sees that tempting Jesus with comfort is like a fat goat offering leftover wheat husks to a lion, he rapidly changes his tactics. Next he offers Jesus acceptance.

If you do this miraculous thing then imagine the attention you would receive." Can you hear the approval and acceptance of the world in this offer—the conditional acceptance that most of us mistake for love? Yet, does this sound like any offer worth pursuing in relation to the unconditional love of God? "This is my Son, the Beloved, with whom I am well pleased." Satan says, "All these things will I give you, if you will fall down and worship me. (Matthew 4:9)

Finally, Satan pulls out all the stops. This is the final offer of Satan. This is his biggest gun.

Do you notice that each offer has a conditional statement built into it, an "if, then"? The first two statements deal with the essence of our Lord's being: "If you are the Son of God . . ." Didn't Jesus already receive that blessing? Wasn't our Lord already God's beloved? Satan was trying to make Jesus doubt the beloved blessing. Yet the last temptation is a different type of condition: "All these things will I give you, if you will fall down and worship me." Those things Satan is talking about are you and me. Satan speaks about us as if we were dead roly-poly bugs under the garbage can, and, indeed, to him that is exactly what we are. If he can't use us, he will toss us aside. Remember, he is not seeking to be in relationship with us. He doesn't want to know our names. He wants to use us and discard us and see if he can hurt God in the process. We are of no value to him unless we can further his goals.

Can you see these hoofprints of Satan in our culture? Can you detect his presence in the way we treat one another individually, corporately, globally? Whenever we treat beings like things, or place a higher value on what someone has or does over their inherent dignity as a child of God, then we too are duped by the Deceiver. The longing for acceptance that is at the core of adolescence is more than a chronological issue. It is a spiritual issue. It is a spiritual battle. It is an unholy vacuum that calls to be filled by God alone, and anything else is a deception.

Here is the greatest sorrow of the battle: "We always seek the acceptance of the one who is least likely to give it"—at least until we can find acceptance at a deeper core. It is hidden in the actions of the parent who gave only conditional acceptance to his sons, whom those boys try forever to please. It is the rejection of the parent who never thought her daughter was "good enough" that drives the daughter to look continually for approval from external sources.

I remember mentioning to a class of youth in detention that I was going to stop by the jail that evening. Over half the class of forty kids asked me to see a dad, uncle, or older brother behind those bars. The kids wanted me to tell their role models, "Tell him I am going to get out. Tell him that I'll do better."

I said to a few of the kids individually, "If you write a letter, I will see if the guard will let me take it in." But each youth responded in kind by saying: "No, he wouldn't read it anyway. He would never listen to me. He thinks I am no good."

I wish you could have seen the sorrow on those kid's faces. I wish you could have heard the pain in their voices. Yet I detect that you might have already experienced this pain somewhere in your life as well, through the eyes of someone who has been conditional in your life—maybe even through the eyes in your own mirror this morning. Still, could you imagine, if we were able to pre-empt this conditional message of Satan? If we could offer a greater blessing—a beloved blessing—that would exceed the "if, then" of the Prince of Lies?

We can, in fact, pre-empt KataDiabolos. That is, in fact, the mission we are given by God. This is the predestined point of our lives—or, better put—the reason we were made. We are to experience this great mercy of God's beloved blessing and then become that blessing to others. We are to go to the very least of these and give them that kind of unconditional love, acceptance without conditions, unconditional blessing. We are created for this work, and if we do not act on it, we will never find the true nature of joy.

The type of love we are called to offer was known to the Greeks as agape. If you did a word search through the Bible, you would find that the noun for *agape* is used over 120 times in the New Testament alone. The verb, *agapao,* is used another 140 times.

There was no greater love than agape love. It was a self-sacrificing love, an "I would die for you" love. It was the love of Jesus when he laid down his life for us, and the love of God when God sent Jesus to lay that life down. It is our greatest commission—the new commandment of Jesus Christ—to "Love one another. Just as I have loved you, you also should love one another" (John 13:34).

But, lest we confuse the contemporary notion of *love* with the Gospel term, agape love really means, "to lay your life down for others as I have laid my life down for you."

Can we accept that God loves us like this? Can we turn around and offer that depth of love to all young people no matter their circumstances? Can we help them experience the depth of God's beloved blessing? This is not a preachy type of love; this is a "being with" love—a "dying for" love. What greater mission in all of life could there possibly be than to fulfill this command of Jesus's? If we can help young people find that kind of acceptance, then we are enabling young people to be manipulation-proof. That is the best "if, then" offer we will ever hear—ever!

Me-otheism

Did you notice that all Satan's temptations were not only conditional but also dealt with self-focus? How would Jesus feel if he changed the rocks into bread? How would Jesus feel if the crowds adored him? What would Jesus get if he just bowed to Satan? In an earlier chapter, we said that we only get by giving. We feel loved when we love. We know peace when we bring peace into the chaos of others' lives. Satan's temptations focus on trying to get Jesus to focus on his own need for approval or acceptance, Jesus's need for love or self-esteem. However, the entire focus of Jesus is on God:

It is written

"One does not live by bread alone,
　but by every word that comes from the mouth of God."

(Matthew 4:4)

Again it is written, "Do not put the Lord your God to the test.'" (Matthew 4:7)

For it is written,
　"Worship the Lord your God,
　and serve only him."

(Matthew 4:10)

Jesus knows he will not be filled full by self-focus but only by worshiping God. Our Lord's sole focus is on God and his commission to serve the least of these. The lack of self-focus by Jesus is enlightening; in fact, it is liberating.

Humility is Christ's answer to Satan's temptations. Not the type of humility that leads to false martyrdom or self-loathing, but the type of humility that leads to dependence upon the cross and the joy that Jesus—the beloved of God—would give everything to share eternity with you and me.

The ultimate life or the beloved life has nothing to do with self-focus. It is a life focused on God and esteeming what God values—service—especially to the least of these. That is the type of fulfill-ment that is produced by humility, not by self-focus. It is the humility that results from true repentance, a repentance that leads to the deep-est joy of liberating service.

There is a purpose to repentance in our lives when it encourages a refocus on God, when it promotes a humility with others, and when it reaffirms the gift of God's ultimate mercy. "For God so loved the world that he gave his only Son" (John 3:16).

To the extent that we can experience this type of God-focus and abandon the self-focus of our culture, we will be liberated. We will be set free from painfully clamoring to fill our own cups and, instead, be available to pour forth into the lives of others. This is the type of liberation we need in order to be available to offer the next genera-tion the beloved blessing of Christ. This is where the heart of true joy lives. Let's reject the deception of Satan that leads us to believe we can find any worthwhile joy in self-centeredness or any authentic fulfillment in self-focus. Instead, let's reveal to others the agape joy of giving—making ourselves a living sacrifice—by leading others to places where the need is great and "setting them free to wash the feet of others."

A New Name

One of the greatest joys of mentoring at detention centers is when an adult mentor approaches me and says, "I never thought I could make such a difference!" Suddenly ordinary people—retirees, housewives, working stiffs like me—become hooked on giving. They want to spend more time in juvey, they want to go to court with these kids, meet their families, take them to movies, and even invite them to be a part of their own family. The poor, the forgotten, the vulnerable are no longer just banal clichés to them; instead, they have taken on a human form with dreams and hopes and names. They experience the inexpressible glory of Christ's Gospel firsthand.

Jesus said, "He has anointed me to bring good news to the poor" (Luke 4:18). I have had the distinct privilege in my life of hearing average people tell me: "The poor cross the street to tell me their good news. They see me coming and call me friend. They ask for me by name."

Talk about the heart of the Gospel, talk about the greatest of joys. It is in these moments when we change the name of the poor to beloved and change our own names to good news. It happens the moment we are willing to leave ourselves behind and take the Gospel of Jesus Christ forward.

A garden outreach project that was started in my community to help kids pay off large community fines. Some of these fines easily exceed $10,000, and if the youth don't make weekly payments on those fines, they risk being incarcerated again. The garden outreach started with five kids and a quarter acre of land. It doesn't sound like much, but it was all manual labor on ground that had previously been nothing but stubborn Bermuda grass. I can remember pulling up clumps that came complete with souvenirs from Australia (the root system was so deep). Each row was 125 feet long in a garden that was 92 feet wide. The object of this outreach was to give the young people their own business and to work the land with them to help them succeed. I and many others walk alongside these kids to help them get their products to market. Any money they make goes toward their community fines, and they also get a little spending money.

It humbles me to see how hard these kids work for their crops, especially when they first began to see the little seeds start to grow. We spent many afternoons together in over 100-degree heat, hoeing with all our strength at weeds that seemed to grow stronger the more we fought with them. One day I was hoeing with my fourteen-year-old friend Lenny. It was one of the hottest days we had spent in the garden, and we were hacking away at crabgrass, wondering if we were really growing vegetables, just growing weeds, or feeding rabbits. Lenny and I simply had chopped our way through about 120 feet of the wretched grass that was growing between our peppers and our tomatoes when he turned to me and said, "Guess what day tomorrow is?"

Of course, I thought, it must be his birthday. "Nope," he replied. "Guess again."

I guessed my way through his entire family before I said: "Lenny, I give up. What day is tomorrow?"

"It's the one-year anniversary of my dad's suicide."

The words hit me like the house that landed on the Wicked Witch of the East. My toes curled up just like her striped socks as I tried to digest how to respond to an anniversary filled with such remorse and sorrow. I leaned on my hoe and just looked at Lenny as he continued to work, covered with sweat, baking in the sun, four feet left in our 125-foot row. It took him 120 feet out of 125 to tell me about what was probably the most defining day in his life to that point. It had ripped his family apart—four children, no mother present, all the kids now in different foster homes.

He said it again: "It's the one-year anniversary of my dad's suicide."

All I could say was: "That must still hurt a lot, Lenny. Do you get to talk about it much?"

That's what Lenny treasured: someone who would be consistent with him during the most inconsistent time of his life, someone who would be there long enough for him to offer his story. What a humbling honor! I would hoe a thousand more 125-foot rows to earn that type of trust again. I constantly ask myself, "Am I willing to hoe the 120 feet of weeds necessary before kids like Lenny will open up their deepest hurts?"

In the story of the disciples who followed Jesus into the wilderness (see John 1:29–41), do you remember how the two young men never approached Jesus? They just walked a few yards behind him. Were they whispering to each other? "You talk to him." "No, you talk to him, you're older." "I'm not going to talk to him!"

How long did they walk behind Jesus whispering to each other before our Lord finally turned around and asked them: "What do you seek?" "What do you value?"

How long was it before they asked, "Master, where do you live (Dear Jesus, we have nothing else, will you let us just spend our lives with you)?"

Was it 10 feet? 20 feet? 121 feet?

Whatever the distance, will we make ourselves available to walk it so that we too might hear the precious words, "Guess what tomorrow is . . . ?"

All our greatest joys in life begin somewhere around that proverbial 120 feet. Somewhere around that distance a person feels safe enough to reveal her or his true heart, her or his real hurt and pain. Somewhere around 120 feet we learn the person's true name. "My name is pain, abandonment, loss of a loved one. . . . Will you walk with me while I try to find my new name?"

I Will Give You a New Name

During the years that I have worked with street youth and youth involved with gangs, I have found that I could rarely change a life on the street. I could be a friend out there. I could be available and present to such young people and even engage in many meaningful conversations, but the allure of the street or the gang life was always too strong for me to reach through that veil. However, at the moment a crisis hits (a young person is arrested, sent to jail, or admitted to the hospital), at that moment, a young person's whole world falls apart. He or she is isolated and alone. The friends that used to be there disappear into the woodwork like bugs running for cover when the kitchen light comes on. Many of us also abandon kids at that point. We don't want those kids around our kids or in our programs. However, that is precisely the most important time that we need to step into a young person's life. The best time to change a life is when the old ideologies or paradigms no longer work. The best way to reach a young person is to be consistent, especially when he or she have been inconsistent.

These are the times when Satan steps in to do his most effective work. He coats a kid like this with the failures of the past. He gives her or him a name based upon failures and sorrows. You can see the young person struggling with this, asking, "Why am I so stupid?" "Why do I always fail?" "I will never be any good to anyone."

But isn't this the time God is most willing to step into our lives?

You shall no more be termed Forsaken,
    and your land shall no more be termed Desolate;
but you shall be called My Delight Is in Her,
    and your land Married;
for the LORD delights in you,
    and your land shall be married

(Isaiah 62:4)

Here is where God changes our names. While Satan would love to skulk around in our shadows, bite at our heels, and burden us with the names "forsaken" and "desolate," our Lord renames us "my delight," and "my beloved."

"This is 'my beloved' in whom I find 'my delight.'"

Read that again, only this time, look into the mirror and say, "I am God's beloved in whom God finds delight."

"Beloved" and "betrothed." Our God is the one who calls us by these new names. They are not names based upon our failures or successes (at least what our culture considers successes). They are not names we are given conditionally based upon our performance or possessions. It is Satan who wants to name us by those stipulations—that is the trait of his conditional approval or acceptance. God names us knowing our greatest longing. God has walked the 120 feet of weeds with us to hear our deepest cries. God is willing to walk as far as it takes or wait as long as it takes to bring us into joy, God's delight. God does not name us based upon what we do or have but based upon what we can become when we are guided by the Holy Spirit.

Stop today and consider this question: "Who do you know who needs to be named 'beloved' today?"

5 Liberating Young People from Their Culture

Then Jesus asked him, "What is your name?" He replied, "My name is Legion, for we are many." (Mark 5:9)

Caught Up in Chaos

The e-mail was waiting when I checked my messages in the morning. A fourteen-year-old named Thomas had been arrested for a drug-related murder. He was part of a local gang of "wanna-bes" that had been trying to push the boundaries of their turf. Apparently, they had tried to steal some chemicals to concoct methamphetamines and wound up in a fight with rival gang members. At 2:30 in the morning, a young man lay dead, and Thomas was being held for murder while his friends had scattered into hiding.

When I first sat down with Thomas, I thought I would be there for about twenty minutes. I just wanted to let him know who I was and that he could talk to me if he had the need. Usually, I don't stay very long on the first visit—just long enough to hopefully leave a young person wanting more. He asked if I would come back the next day, so I did, and he told me that he wanted to come clean.

He told me how shameful he felt, and I wanted to learn what it was that he regretted. I wanted to find out if he was sorry that he was caught or sorry that he had taken another person's life.

Thomas began to tell me about the night of the murder, beginning with the fight, but I asked him to go even further back for me. "What happened before you showed up to take the chemicals?" I asked. He told me they were just driving around and talking about "doing something" that night. I then asked, "What happened before that?"

"I was home smoking weed," he said. "I was bored." I cannot tell you how many young people tell me they felt bored before they got into trouble.

"Did you call your friends, Thomas? Did you go looking for them? Did they come to find you?"

"No," Thomas replied, "I was just hanging out on the street. They came by and told me to go with them."

"Thomas," I pushed a little harder, "why did you get in that car?"

"I don't know," Thomas looked me straight in the face and tears welled up in his eyes. "I feel so stupid, so scared. I don't know why I got in that car."

"When you say you feel stupid and scared, what does that mean, Thomas?"

"I feel scared, Jerry, because no one will ever see me the same again. Everyone knows I helped murder someone. Everyone sees me as a murderer. I'm scared for what will happen to me—not just now—but forever, Jerry. I know I may be in prison for a long time, but am I going to hell too?"

Before we dealt with that question, I asked: "Thomas, you said you felt stupid as well. What do you mean by *stupid*?"

"I knew I should have never stepped into that car. I knew it. I could sense it, Jerry, like someone was tapping me on the shoulder and saying, 'Don't do this, Thomas.' Then, I did it anyway. I did it anyway, Jerry! Now, look what happened. I was stupid. I was afraid. I was afraid they would hassle me, maybe even beat me up. I didn't want them to think I was scared. Now look what I have done!"

I was convinced that Thomas was truly repentant (to the degree that he was able to comprehend his actions as a fourteen-year-old raised with little or no parameters in his life). So many of the young people I see who wind up incarcerated in our penal system talk to me as if they were merely observers in a first-person-shooter video game. They talk about watching themselves commit the crime and wondering why they are doing it even while they are doing it. Many have experiences like Thomas, where they actually feel warned not to go somewhere or not to spend time with someone. That warning, I believe, comes from the Holy Spirit, but so few young people (and adults) know how to attune to the Holy Spirit, that the experience passes them by in the chaos of the moment. They make bad choices—horrific choices—choices that alter their lives or even end them. And why? Because they hunger so desperately to be accepted, and they fear rejection so deeply.

Then, KataDiabolos raises his hideous head and says: "That's you, 'scared and stupid.' That's your true name."

Our Crosses and Our Thomases

As I have mentioned before, we are not surprised by violence today; we are only surprised when it happens to us. Though we are not surprised by the stories of people like Thomas, we should be. These types of actions should shock and anger and propel us into action. We are losing a generation, but not to violence. Violence is only a symptom. We are losing a generation to abandonment. That's the deeper social ill. The Thomases of our world use violence, not just as a form of resolving frustration but as a means of gaining acceptance. One of the major ways for a male to join a gang is to find an innocent person and beat them up. The gang leader might say, "Go to the mall and beat up an old woman." He might demand that the young initiate, "Take this bat and beat up a jock at school," or, "Drug that girl and bring her to my motel room."

The young person does it. Why? It is not because of personal anger or lust at the person whom they victimize. It is not just for the thrill. It is for acceptance from the gang and its leader, to be a part of the group. And at the root of that acceptance is abandonment. What if we could pre-empt that cry for recognition? I think of Thomas (and all the Thomases I have met in my work), and I can't stop asking, "What if I had been there ten minutes earlier than that car of 'wanna-bes'?"

This was the primary reason I started a mentoring outreach program for at-risk youth. This outreach is not as much a program as it is a conversation. It is completely reliant upon an adult spending an hour a week with one youth and encouraging that young person to talk about things that really matter to him or her. It is simply about engaging a young person in a relevant conversation and really listening to him or her. How complex is that? The young people love their time with these adults. For many of these young people, it is more quality time with an adult than they have had in a year, maybe even years. They are so used to hearing commands—"get up," "clean your room," "go to bed"—that conversation is alien to them. It may be the first time a healthy adult has sat down and listened to them for an hour without being paid. The young people ask the guards, "When are the 'happy people' coming in (that's what they call us)?" They seek continued relationships with their mentors after their release. They ask their mentors to go to court with them, talk to their parents with them, see the probation officer with them.

This is how we franchise disenfranchised youth. This is how we engage disengaged children. We call them friends by giving them our two most valuable commodities—time and attention.

Demons in Our Midst

> When he saw Jesus from a distance, he ran and bowed down before him, and he shouted at the top of his voice, "What have you to do with me, Jesus, Son of the Most High God? I adjure you by God, do not torment me." For he had said to him, "Come out of the man, you unclean spirit!" Then Jesus asked him, "What is your name?" He replied, "My name is Legion; for we are many." He begged him earnestly not to send them out of the country. Now there on the hillside a great herd of swine was feeding, and the unclean spirits begged him, "Send us into the swine, let us enter them." So he gave them permission. And the unclean spirits came out and entered the swine; and the herd, numbering about two thousand, rushed down the steep bank into the sea, and were drowned in the sea. (Mark 5:6–13)

What do you observe in this reading? Did you notice that the first thing that Jesus does upon his arrival in the Gerasenes is follow a demon-possessed man straight to a graveyard (remember, at that time, no self-respecting rabbi would be found with the Gerasenes, in a graveyard, or with a demon-possessed man). To that man—that least likely of characters, that least deserving person—Jesus takes God's blessing.

We will return to a number of things about this reading in future chapters, but right now, it is important to note two amazing aspects of our Lord's behavior from this reading:

• Wherever the day finds Jesus, he finds the most lost, most forgotten, and most alienated and makes them family.

- One man was more important to Jesus than two-thousand pigs, yet, even more than that, one man was worth more to our Lord than a whole region's economy!

Does that sound similar to our attitude as followers of the Way? Are we constantly seeking the least of these no matter where the day leads us (even if we are way off our course)? Are we willing to spend everything on earth to buy back one person for heaven? How does that sound for a Sunday homily? "Go, and wherever you find yourself this week, seek the alienated and buy them back by any means into the love of your God."

The demons of our culture are present not in our economy but in the way we worship our economy. Our cultural norms are backward from the ways of Jesus. To Jesus, the economy existed to bring home the lost, especially the most lost. He used things to redeem people. However, our culture sees people as things, measuring them not by their dignity, but by their productivity.

This includes their productivity in our personal lives. Too often we plan our week by who can further our interests or which contacts will enhance our career. Compare the questions "Who is the most important person I can see this week?" and "Who is the most important person that needs Christ's love this week?" Will the first question lead us closer to our family? Will the first question lead us closer to the alienated? Will the first question lead us closer to Jesus?

In fact, the first question leads us to one further question that often prevents us from hearing the call of the Holy Spirit: "What have you done for me lately?"

The demons of our culture take root in this question. It precludes us from becoming spiritually mature and makes us increasingly self-focused and decreasingly self-sacrificing. Our hearts harden around these consumer contexts until we see the actions of Jesus as a threat to our economy (just as the Gerasenes did). So, what do we do? We make Jesus into our image. Many churches create a consumer gospel, a personal gospel that focuses on entertainment and feeling good—theatrical, emotionally-charged worship events that are filled with live bands and streaming videos but turn a blind eye to the suffering within blocks of our churches.

It is deceptive because we wave our hands, sing loudly, and talk profusely about God, so we feel like we are actually worshiping our Creator. However, the worship ends with "Are you right with Jesus?"

and not "Have you been to the graveyards of the Gerasenes this week?"

But look at the rest of the story. The great news is that the Gerasenes actually change because of a witness Jesus leaves with them. Look what happens—it is one of the greatest stories of evangelism in the Bible:

> As he was getting into the boat, the man who had been possessed by demons begged him that he might be with him. But Jesus refused, and said to him, "Go home to your friends, and tell them how much the Lord has done for you, and what mercy he has shown you." And he went away and began to proclaim in the Decapolis how much Jesus had done for him, and everyone was amazed. (Mark 5:18–20)

The man (formerly known as Legion) pleads to go with Jesus, but Jesus sends him back to his own people to share the Good News. But wait! How much training did that man have? How much of the Scriptures had he studied? How much time had he spent with the religious? None! He had been a demoniac, chased away, beaten, chained by his own people—and those are the very people to whom Jesus sends him back. He has no mastery of the Scriptures, ritual, or tradition. All he has is this: "You know what I was, and you see what I am now. Jesus did this for me."

Who does that sound like? The Samaritan woman at the well? "He knows everything that I have done and still loves me!"

In that statement we can find all the testimony any of us need to evangelize the world, especially the consumer-based world that treats its wounded so harshly. "You know what I was, and you see what I am now. Jesus did this for me."

The man simply shares what Jesus did in his life, and who can deny the change? Who can deny the miraculous transformation? The Gerasenes begin to long for that kind of change even more than they longed to keep their pigs intact.

Imagine having an impact like this on a culture that once cared more about its pigs than its people, using only the simple words: "You know what I was. Now look at what Jesus did to me." The man (formerly known as Legion) became one of the greatest and earliest "apostles of Jesus" (remember *disciple* means "follow and learn," while *apostle* means "commissioned and sent"). Are we ready to take the simple message of the unschooled man (formerly known as Legion) and spread it to a culture that values things more than beings?

Consumerism

Remember that KataDiabolos can prevent us from a mature faith by keeping the focus on ourselves, our acceptance, seducing us into using others toward our own ends and justifying the means. His whispers can be found in two horrible half-truths that keep our culture diseased.

Consumerism is rooted in two biblically false premises: (1) The more you have, the happier you are; and (2) The more you have or do, the more important you are.

Based upon those parameters, we begin to believe that a person's worth is a product of what she or he has or does. Valuable people either have or do a lot, but those who do not have or cannot do are worthless. In particular, we begin to judge people's worth by what they can do for us or how they can increase what we have. If that thought is carried out across a culture, then the emphasis of that culture is to free ourselves from those who would encumber us from getting or doing more. Who fits into that category—the category of what we might call the "encumberers"?

Consider the question we often ask our elderly: "So, tell me, what were you?" Would it not be reasonable for an elderly person to respond: "What was I *when*? You mean I am not *now*?"

In a like manner, what do we ask our youth? "So, tell me, what are you going to be?" Their legitimate response (were they able to formulate it) might well be, "*When* am I going to be?"

At a time when their hunger to belong and their need for identity is at its apex, young people often do not experience belongingness or identity in our culture. They are the "church of tomorrow," the "future church," but in no way do we treat them like God treated Jeremiah:

> Then I said, "Ah, Lord GOD! Truly I do not know how to speak, for I am only a boy." But the LORD said to me,
>> "Do not say, 'I am only a boy';
>> for you shall go to all to whom I send you,
>> and you shall speak whatever I command you."
>
> (Jeremiah 1:6–7)

Our youth are ready for just such a mission and just such a challenge, but all too often they are instead trapped in a form of enforced "consumer purgatory" that keeps increasing on both ends. They are "humans becoming, humans that will be—someday." So, what do we do with them in the meantime? We institutionalize them.

We send them out to fend for themselves at earlier and earlier ages with increasing demands and decreasing resources. Sadly, our children do not have a voting block to stop the unfunded mandates that plague their situation (at least the elderly have one of the strongest voting blocks in our nation), so their class sizes increase, their interaction with positive adult role models dwindles, and their dependency upon one another is amplified. They hungrily seek approval from one another and less often seek the approval of adults.

Too often the institutional response to our children or our elderly (or mentally or physically disabled) is to manage them, not engage them. Our government spends more of its resources on fueling the special interests of corporations and less resources on those at the fringe of the economy—more on those who have and do and less on those who don't. In such an economy, things are more important than people, and we judge people's value by their things. We become like the Gerasenes, valuing our pigs more than our people.

There is no other way to describe this than demonic. It is the antithesis of God's values that always challenge us to feed those who are hungry, visit those who are incarcerated, care for those who are widowed or orphaned, and welcome those who are strangers. We wonder why corporations and governments have ethical problems, but we don't recognize the core of the problem—to maximize profit at all costs because profit, not people, equals value.

What Have You Done for Me Lately?

The demon of consumerism has an impact not just socially but also personally. Relationships are guided by the question mentioned earlier in this chapter: "What have you done for me lately?"

This creates relationships that are valued by whether someone is of use to us. If we can use someone, we will be in relationship with him or her. If we can't use someone, we don't want anything to do with him or her. However, this isn't relationship; it is manipulation. Manipulation is when we have an ulterior motive to our relationship and use others to get what we want. That is the very definition of the approval or acceptance bias of our culture. "I will accept you if you can further my career or contacts." Or, for our kids, "If you do what we do, you can be who we are."

There is no possible way this type of bias can lead to real love or real community. This manipulation is at the heart of our culture's inability to form community. Community cannot occur without commitment, and how can we commit to someone if we don't know how long she or he will be useful to us? That is exactly how long our relationships last. Not "til death do us part," but instead "'til you are no longer useful to me."

One day, in the middle of an after-school program, I recognized the "hidden statistics" of our culture. That night I sat down and wrote a song about three of the kids I had met that day:

"Hidden Statistics"

Verse I

Stevie is an eight-year-old. He never asked for much,
His father left when he was three and still is out of touch.
He has a little brother, but he's sick most of the time.
It's so hard to keep your dreams alive when your life's been so unkind.
Jasmine is a prostitute—that's not her real name.
She's lived in concrete-jungles most her life, you can bet she knows the games.
She looks to be 'bout thirty, though last week she turned sixteen,
And she doesn't stand much chance at all of seeing seventeen.

Chorus

They're just some of the hidden statistics. Faces we've never seen.
They're the blinder side of justice, a challenge we won't meet.
And we know, they are different from other boys and girls,
But their face doesn't count for much, in such a crazy grown-up world.

Verse II

Rosalie is Latino, her parents work the fields.
The meager funds they make buy a room and simple meals.

Her education is suffering because her English is not good.
She tries so hard but she can't keep up—there's no way she really could.

Chorus

They're just some of the hidden statistics. Faces we've never seen.
They're the blinder side of justice, a challenge we won't meet.
And we know, they are different from other boys and girls,
But their face doesn't count for much, in such a crazy grown-up world.

Refrain

Who speaks for these children, who stands for their rights?
Who cherishes their broken dreams, who will comfort them tonight?
Who speaks for these children, and if it isn't you and me,
That is standing strong on their behalf, tell me please,
Who will it be?

Chorus

They're just some of the hidden statistics. Faces we've never seen.
They're the blinder side of justice, a challenge we won't meet.
And we know, they are different from other boys and girls,
But their face doesn't count for much, in such a crazy grown-up world.

Who will take up the cross for the young people who are our "hidden statistics"? Who will stand up for them? If not us, who?

When a culture is built upon "utilitarian relationships," those who can get ahead and take us with them become the leaders. It matters not how many are left behind—as long as we are not one of them. Biblical leadership, however, is not about how far we can get ahead but whether we left anyone behind.

The Spirit of the Lord is upon me,
    because he has anointed me,
        to bring good news to the poor.

He has sent me to proclaim release to the captives
  and recovery of sight to the blind,
    to let the oppressed go free,
to proclaim the year of the Lord's favor.

(Luke 4:18)

If that was the mission of Jesus Christ, shouldn't it also be our mission as his followers? Yet Christ's mission statement is counter to a consumer culture. To bring "Good News to the poor," release those who are in captivity, help those who cannot see, set free those who are oppressed, and "to proclaim the year of the Lord's favor" means nothing other than to level the economic playing field to include everyone.

My dearest friends, I must tell you that I am hopelessly in love with Jesus Christ. I am completely foolish in the eyes of this culture and completely in love with those whom God has allowed me to serve as a missionary. Please allow me to let that serve as the consumer warning label for this book. Given that precursor, let me go on to say that there is no greater joy in life than to be a "fool for Christ," to lose yourself in love for those whom he called the "least of these." There is no finer purpose, no higher cause, and no sweeter feeling than to be surrounded by those who call you "Good News" because they have been released from an emotional, spiritual, or physical captivity (incarceration, intimidation, or victimhood). What a joy it is to see those who were blind or who lacked vision begin to see that they can impact their world, or those who were oppressed become liberated from disabling systems or relationships. We are called and commissioned to seek out those youth who are most alienated and least accepted and bring them to the table.

Challenging the Belief System

Young people live in a vacuum of values and meaning that was passed on to them when they were made second-rate citizens in a consumer society. We can tinker with their system, but unless we change the culture, it is all just cosmetic.

This systemic change cannot be reached by merely changing the system or the programs within it. Our undervalued youth need relationships with caring and consistent adults who will bless them with the very personal words of our Creator: "This is my Son, the Beloved, with whom I am well pleased."

For example, improving our education system alone will not be enough to prepare our kids for the world they are inheriting. High test scores alone don't ensure the ability to communicate or motivate self or others. High test scores will not create an ethic of cooperation in a world that is being divided by fanatical religious groups (Christians and others alike). We need to challenge the cultural beliefs that state that things are more important than people, right down to the relational level.

I think of conversations I have heard kids have with one another regarding sex when they didn't know I was listening: "Did you get some? Did you do it?" Even, "Did you do her or him?" I challenge the adolescent males in our programs, "Do you see that young woman as God's daughter or as your toy?" Increasingly, that principle now applies both ways across the gender divide when sex just becomes another way to score.

How do we teach our young people that things serve beings and that every human being, even someone we consider an enemy, has dignity in that he or she was created by God? How do we show them that it is never proper to use others to get what we want? How do we teach our young people that ends never justify the means if the means involve manipulation? How do we show them that if we don't control the means, we cannot control the ends? For example, getting an A does not justify cheating on a test. Do we stress out about their grades or their effort? What are we most concerned about—their sports scores or their initiative and effort? their competitive nature or their cooperative endeavors? The test is far less important than sacrificing integrity for a higher grade. How can we model that value as a community leader or as a mentor, ensuring that the most alienated have their feet washed too.

We need to get to the heart of the problem. Right down to changing the subtle language we use with youth. Can you imagine how different their responses would be "Whom do you admire and how do we become like them?" and "What qualities are important to you and how do we grow them?" instead of "What are you going to be . . . someday?"

Our Thomases are trapped in a user-friendly world, a world that is friendly to users. He was a perfect setup to be manipulated. His low sense of value, his lack of purpose, his need for acceptance—all these things helped put Thomas in prison for years. Will this day find us with kids like him? The heart of the problem must lead us to examine even our own consumption habits. Where would we fit in the Gerasene picture? Would we be with the villagers—angry and afraid of the Messiah who threw away our "things" to save one "being"? Or, maybe we would be the man (formerly called Legion) who runs house to house offering the beloved blessing by telling others: "You know what I was—now look who I am. It was all because of Jesus."

6 Gospel Authenticity

"Father if you are willing, remove this cup from me, yet, not my will but yours be done." (Luke 22:42)

Pathways to a Life of Blessing

Who sets up a young person for success or failure, not in this world's eyes but in God's eyes? Teaching any desired behavior requires two critical tasks: (1) modeling the desired result so the recipient can experience it; and (2) clarifying the desired result in a manner that the recipient can grasp it.

Are we literate enough in the language of God to define what success or failure looks like in our Creator's eyes? Are we capable of expressing those terms in a manner that a young person, just forming cognitive pathways, can grasp them?

The term *cognitive pathways* is fairly new to the field of adolescent development and has largely been developed because of advancements in the field of neuroscience. It is an extremely complex field, and being that I am neither a brain surgeon nor a rocket scientist, I thought I would offer you one of the simplest definitions of *cognitive pathways* that I have stumbled upon:

> In the past, many health experts have attributed the turmoil years of adolescence to hormonal changes that start during puberty. While sudden surges in hormones may account for some of the problem, experts say there is much more going on in the adolescent body.
>
> Researchers have found the brain undergoes some significant changes during adolescence. From 13 to 15, the brain increases in

size. Improvement is seen in areas of the brain responsible for motor skills and spatial perception. Memory and learning are at their peak. The brain is beginning to develop pathways that regulate emotion and cognitive function. Those new pathways grow out of experience. That's why adolescents feel they need to engage in new behaviors. Unfortunately, the frontal lobe, or area of the brain responsible for reasoning and judgment, doesn't develop until later in adolescence—often not until 17 or older. So adolescents may engage in risky behaviors without being able to fully understand the consequences of their actions.

(Medstar Television, Teen Brain, May 11, 2005)

As adults we have learned neural shortcuts or pathways for dealing with issues in our lives. Those pathways are like shortcuts through the high stalks of a wheat field. The more we take a specific shortcut, the more that pathway is worn down. These pathways aid us in decision making so that when we are confronted by an issue we don't have to weigh through multiple options in order to respond quickly.

However, these pathways can also become ruts that lock us into destructive behaviors. Most of the recovering alcoholics I have known in our jail outreaches were given alcohol by a male authority figure somewhere around the age of twelve. At that point they began to see alcohol as the best pathway to receive approval and acceptance, and eventually they generalized the rush of alcohol or drugs to include them as the optimal ways to deal with stress or chaos in their lives.

Cognitive pathway theories continue to offer us understanding into the development of both healthy and unhealthy behavior among youth. The most obvious implications of pathway theories in our field are that youth develop a pathway before they develop the cognitive justification of their actions. That should have an incredible impact on values and religious education that involve young people. We often attempt to put concepts into their heads before the youth can practice them in their hearts. Being intelligent creatures, we can repeat back what we have heard, but information that is not tied to behavior is impertinent. We haven't learned it—we just remember it.

To learn, we need to put the concepts we wish to convey into practice and then say to young people: "Look, here is what you did. This is what happened." Then we see the astonishment on their faces—the Gestalt moment: "Oh that's what you mean. I get it now."

We can put whatever we want to in their brains, but it won't make a difference until they put their beliefs into practice. Only by creating "pathways to God" and "pathways to my neighbor" can young people begin to learn that faith is indeed the most significant response to the challenges and joys of life.

A few months ago, I was asked to give a Christian leadership retreat for young people in a Michigan Catholic high school. Instead of starting out with a list of techniques, I asked the youth, "What is the most pressing issue for youth in your schools or in this county?"

"Drugs!" was the adamant response.

"Would you like to stop drugs before they become a problem in young people's lives?" I asked. Of course the young people said yes.

"Why do you think kids take drugs?" I asked the group. Without any prompting, the students agreed that most everyone they knew who used drugs had a huge need for acceptance and approval. Those kids then decided that the best time to reach kids with a message of unconditional acceptance and "God's approval" was when they were really young. I asked them, "Where are the youngest kids near here?" They told me there was a grade school within two blocks of their high school.

By the afternoon, the youth had called the principal of that grade school to ask about starting a reading program with children in the school who were having behavioral problems. The high-school students would go in once a week to read one-on-one with children in the kindergarten class. They had also talked to the principal of their high school who thought it was a great idea and would see if he could get them released from class and appoint an advisor to the group so they could be credited for their effort. The young people decided to do the activity at the end of the school day so they could go out for a snack afterward and support one another in their efforts to stop drugs before they start.

The next day we talked about the concepts of Christian leadership. The young people reflected on the steps they took—recognizing a problem, seeking its root source, mobilizing around a vision, developing an action plan, and putting it into practice. With each step the youth said: "Oh yea! That's like when we called the principal. Hey, that's like when we wrote down our tasks and assigned them to different people."

This is how young people learn to lead and establish their values. It should also be how they learn about faith.

Imagine taking one of the young people we have mentioned in this book—Christine, Lenny, Thomas—and being there as they were forming their cognitive pathways. Imagine helping them experience the joy of learning: "If I don't feel loved, I can find someone else who needs to be loved and love him or her. If I don't feel understood, I can find another person who needs to be understood and listen to him or her. If I feel bored, I can take the initiative to find a healthy friend and do something creative with him or her. If I feel lonely, I can take the initiative to find a caring adult and ask him or her to listen. If I see a problem, I can be a leader."

Last night in juvenile detention, our mentoring group was engaged with eight kids (six of whom were actively involved in local gangs), and we were discussing the issue of manipulation versus friendship. The local parish youth minister was there mentoring a young lady named Peggy, and he mentioned the concept of living an "authentic life." Peggy asked him, "What is authentic?" My brother-in-Christ summed it up perfectly when he said, "It is when we don't manipulate others and love them unconditionally."

Peggy turned to the entire group, and with the most determined eyes I have ever seen, blurted out: "I want to live like that. I want to live authentically!"

She experienced authenticity in her mentoring relationship with this youth minister. Now she wanted to become authentic with others. She felt it, and now she wants to live it.

What does that tell us precisely? We should be teaching young people to love the Gospel by being the Gospel—until they are at an age where their love compels them to dive deeper into the theology of the Gospel. The desire to know follows the desire to love. For example, most of us learned to read because someone we wanted to impress read to us. We fell in love with being read to long before we fell in love with reading. We need to find more ways to help young people "fall in love with Jesus," not just listen to someone talk about him. They need to experience the joy of the Gospel-centered life if it is going to become an applicable pathway for them in adulthood.

Models of Gospel Authenticity

How able are we to define *Gospel authenticity* to those around us? Every passage of the Scriptures leads us to understand that Gospel authenticity occurs when we are able to move from the selfishness of this world to the selflessness of Jesus.

In John's account of the Last Supper, Jesus abandons all decorum and positional authority to become the servant at the table. He washes the feet of his disciples and tells us what an authentic Christian must do for others.

> After he had washed their feet, had put on his robe, and had returned to the table, he said to them, "Do you know what I have done to you? You call me Teacher and Lord—and you are right, for that is what I am. So if I, your Lord and Teacher, have washed your feet, you also ought to wash one another's feet. For I have set you an example, that you also should do as I have done to you." (John 13:12–15)

In the Garden of Gethsemane, Jesus prays the prayer of ultimate Gospel authenticity when he places his will completely at God's disposal—no matter the cost.

> "Father if you are willing, remove this cup from me, yet, not my will but yours be done." (Luke 22:42)

Despite a life of setbacks and failures, Jesus commissions Peter with the greatest challenge to the Christian life. Here we see *Gospel authenticity* defined as "allowing God to use others to take us even 'where you do not wish to go'."

> "Very truly, I tell you, when you were younger, you used to fasten your own belt and to go wherever you wished. But when you grow old, you will stretch out your hands, and someone else will fasten a belt around you and take you where you do not wish to go." (He said this to indicate the kind of death by which he would glorify God.) After this he said to him, "Follow me." (John 21:18–19)

Jesus certainly modeled this authenticity to his disciples and taught them by walking with them down multiple pathways. That was the Hebrew style of preaching—not in a classroom, not in an assembly hall, not through visual aids and movie clips, but with the simple invitation, "Come and see" (John 1:39). Look at the didactic method here: (1) The disciples fall in love with Jesus; then (2) they fall in love with his message; then (3) they fall in love with its application. I see this happening in our mentoring programs all the time. Hardened kids come in and sit with middle-aged and elderly adults.

They seem to have nothing in common with each other. Yet, in five to ten minutes of listening, those young people have fallen in love with the adults simply because the adults listened to them! Once the adult listens to them, the youth want to share more and hear more. "How do I live an authentic life?"

But what the heck does that mean to a young person struggling for identity? To Peggy it meant that she wanted to exchange the love of the streets for the authentic love of Christ. That's about as near as the Kingdom of heaven can get to us. To teach the Gospel is to invite young people with us to "come and see" how we are joyfully willing to be "bound and sent" and to love like Jesus loved.

"Come and see" is our modus operandi; "bound and sent" is our vocation. These are the themes of Gospel authenticity that we need to set as an ideal to a generation eager for service and dying to be engaged.

In each case the model of Christian authenticity is always to humbly turn over our lives to God in the service of others. It is hard to understand from a worldly perspective how this leads to joy. Yet the greatest joys in life are always selfless, not selfish. Saint Francis of Assisi summed up his prayer of authenticity in one verse:

> My dearest God, who are you? And, who am I but your useless servant? (Spoto, *Reluctant Saint*, p. 154)

It is so difficult for our culture to grasp the absolute freedom of a prayer like that! "My dearest God, who are you?" This part of the prayer indicates a life that is expectantly looking for God's touch in each moment. To Francis, life was like a gift waiting to be unwrapped; he was a man of joyful expectancy. Can we imagine that quality as the cornerstone of our lives? Can we imagine facing each moment with the joyful expectancy of, "God, I can't wait to see what you have in store for me next."

The second stanza of Francis's prayer is even more revealing: "Who am I but your useless servant?" You want to talk about choosing to liberate ourselves of ourselves so that we can serve God more fully each day? With this prayer in our hearts, no person is our competitor. We don't have to struggle to put ourselves above anyone. We are free from the flimsy and false promises of this world of hubris and false pride. Instead, every person has integrity and God is our blessed claim to dignity.

This is the emptying of self and the filling of "the other" that signifies Gospel authenticity. This is the freedom that Jesus offers us. That is the life we want our young people to fall in love with—the authentic life, the life worth living. Are there Peggys in our lives, hungering and eager to learn about authentic love because we authentically love them?

Teaching Gospel Authenticity

Could we define *Gospel authenticity* in a sentence like a mission statement that we could carry with us wherever we went? Would we be tempted to introduce pages of documents underscored by multiple modalities of curriculum objectives? or could we just state it as simply as Jesus did with his disciples? Shortly after washing the disciples' feet, Jesus defines Gospel authenticity to those around him in a new commandment: "I give you a new commandment, that you love one another. Just as I have loved you, you also should love one another" (John 13:34).

Period. That's it. End of sentence. Class is dismissed. "Love others like I loved you."

Can we embrace the unparalleled authenticity of that statement? It is a love beyond selfishness and even a love beyond self. We simply are not capable of loving like that without the aid of the Holy Spirit. Yet, praise God, for even a prostitute can say, "He knows everything I did and still loves me." Even a former demon-possessed man can say: "You know what I was. Now look who I am because Jesus loved me." And Peggy can recognize the difference between manipulation and authenticity and say: "I want to live like that. I want to live authentically." Why can she say that? Because she was loved authentically. She tasted a moment when she was not loved conditionally. She was not loved for what she has, does, or would do for someone; she was loved because she is God's child and that is enough dignity for anyone. If we continue to do our work and Peggy experiences that kind of love on a consistent basis from multiple sources, she will be hard-pressed to go back to a manipulative love. Can you think of any clearer mission for our churches, our ministries, ourselves than to find those who have been manipulated, abused, dispirited, and disheartened and love them like Jesus loves? Look at how our Lord responded to the dispirited:

> When he saw the crowds, he had compassion for them, because they were harassed and helpless, like sheep without a shepherd. Then he said to his disciples, "The harvest is plentiful, but the laborers are few, therefore ask the Lord of the harvest to send out laborers into his harvest." (Matthew 9:36–38)

Are we the Church for which Jesus begged? Have we made it out of the grain elevator and into the harvest yet? Are we waiting for more insight, purer transparency, or deeper authenticity? We don't need to. God doesn't rely on our ability. The more we love, the more authentic we become. There is the greatest beauty. It isn't our past that makes us inauthentic—that's what KataDiabolos wants us to think. Our authenticity lies in admitting our past and repenting from, or rising above, it. Look again at the statements of the woman at the well and the man formerly known as Legion. There is no greater authenticity than saying, "I was a sinner and he loved me too."

God is greater than our sin. If we show the desire to love authentically, God will complete the circle for us in a way that is beyond our ability, surpassing our understanding.

> Rejoice in the Lord always, again I will say, Rejoice. Let your gentleness be known to everyone. The Lord is near. Do not worry about anything, but in everything by prayer and supplication with thanksgiving let your requests be made known to God. And the peace of God, which surpasses all understanding, will guard your hearts and your minds in Christ Jesus. (Philippians 4:4–7)

Look at our roles in this incredible promise of peace: (1) to rejoice; (2) to be known by everyone for our gentleness; and (3) to pray with thanksgiving. How could it get any better than that? This was how that youth minister shared with Peggy and now Peggy wants to be like that with others. She made huge strides into Gospel authenticity even though she is only just learning what that means. The key is she wants to learn! Just like the woman at the well, Peggy finally knows the difference between being authentically loved and being deceitfully manipulated.

From Cultural Immaturity to Gospel Authenticity

When do we move from cultural immaturity to Gospel authenticity? The moment we move from waiting to be loved to loving. When will Peggy become authentically mature? The moment she intentionally takes that step to love others in greater need than herself. At that moment she moves from victim to victor, from helpless to hopeful. Gospel authenticity occurs the moment we move from a life of taking to a life for giving.

I believe that the concept of *forgiveness* is so important that I teach it repeatedly to the young people I encounter—young people like Peggy who have been violated and abandoned most of their short lives. Yet, who among us has not felt manipulated or violated? Who among us hasn't felt anger or betrayal or disappointment?

I can remember sitting with a group of eight teenage males who had been permanently expelled from the school system for their disinterest in education. As we worked through the mentoring session on forgiveness, five of the eight kids in that room related experiences where they had been hit so hard that either teeth were knocked loose or they were knocked unconscious. Each of the kids talked about reporting incidents of violence only to wind up back in the same home and treated worse. Did they have a right to their hurt? Did they have a right to demand change? Did they have a right to be angry that we, their community, did not advocate for them? Yes, yes, and yes! Yet, we must simultaneously move them into wholeness, and wholeness will be found only in forgiveness. I believe that the person who holds on to her or his anger becomes stuck at the onset of that crisis and can never move beyond it until she or he lets go of the anger! Just as an alcoholic's emotional development freezes at the onset of that disease, we become mired in the anger that we cannot displace. We are arrested by self-righteousness, and forgiveness is the great liberator!

It was one of the greatest focal points of Christ's teachings. He tells us:

- To the extent that we forgive, we are forgiven (see Matthew 6:12).
- If we forgive others, God will forgive us (see Matthew 6:14).
- If we do not forgive others, God will not forgive us (see Matthew 6:15).

- It doesn't matter how many times a person sins against us—even if it is seventy-seven times, we must still forgive the repentant sinner (see Matthew 18:22).
- Before we pray to God, we need to make sure we have forgiven others so that we too will be forgiven (see Mark 11:25).
- If we don't judge, we won't be judged; if we don't condemn, we won't be condemned; if we forgive, we will be forgiven (see Luke 6:37).

Jesus knew our emancipation would come from liberating ourselves from anger and encompassing the commission of freeing others from their sin.

Cleanse the Labeled

We know our Lord often felt visceral anger, such as when he overturned the moneychangers' tables in the court of the Gentiles, yet his anger was never self-righteous; it was always an anger of justice and righteousness. The moneychangers and the religious system had made it impossible for the weak, the sick, and the poor to gain access to the inner court of God. They, in collaboration with the high priests, had turned the "house of God" into a "den of robbers" (Matthew 21:13).

Much of our anger is not the righteous anger of Christ seeking justice for the "least of these"; instead, much of our anger is rooted in righteous indignation and a false sense of trust. We trust other people or the Church to be more than it can possibly be and are angry when they disappoint us. We trust our leaders, friends, or spouses to be perfect and are offended when they turn out to be human after all. That is not trust; that is a setup. Jesus trusted people to be true to their character and then called them to live at a higher level.

To live "for giving," we have to get beyond our false expectations of others and meet them in their humanness. We have to quit setting them up. Even more, we have to get beyond righteous indignation and know ourselves for who we are—sinners that Jesus redeemed.

Forgiveness is an alien concept to a culture that speaks consistently in terms of rights and litigates rather than communicates. Though the culture seeks to vilify sinners, the follower of Christ should seek to verify them. Our Lord models this to an unclean woman who tries to sneak some mercy when Jesus is on his way from dining with the tax collectors at Matthew's house to raising a dead child at a religious leader's house (now that's a full evening). The woman who had been hemorrhaging for twelve years touches the back of his robe. She tried to hide in the crowd because she could be stoned if anyone found out she was moving among them. Like lepers, she had to yell, "Unclean!" everywhere she went and keep distant from all gatherings. Would this religious leader (Jesus) stone her?

Jesus makes three substantial statements to this woman in Matthew 9:22: (1) He calls her "daughter." The last time this woman had been included in a family, let alone a community, was at least twelve years prior. Jesus restores her to family; (2) He tells her to "take heart [courage]." Jesus restores her dignity; (3) He says, "Your faith has made you well." Jesus shows her that the power to heal was already inside her, and Jesus was the conduit. She could take that faith anywhere; he didn't even have to be physically present for her to continue to remain whole. Jesus restored her to wholeness. Jesus gave her family, dignity, and an authentic relationship with God.

That is what the parish youth minister gave to Peggy the other day. He made her family, gave her dignity, and showed her how she could also live an authentic life. Jesus says, "Cleanse the lepers" (Matthew 10:8). The "lepers" are the "labeled." Anyone upon whom society puts a label and casts out is a leper. That includes Peggy, Christine, Christopher, and Thomas. That includes those who are homeless and incarcerated, those who are illegal aliens, homosexuals, anyone—anyone—that our society prejudges and calls unclean. "Cleanse the labeled!" "Embrace the outcast."

The bleeding woman didn't find salvation in being just physically healed. She found salvation—authentic restoration—in being sent with the power of God to heal and forgive others. Through Christ, she had the ability to go and tell others: "Your faith can heal you too! I was rejected, unclean, and abandoned for twelve years, and Jesus said 'my faith healed me.' Your faith can heal you too."

We are surrounded by a sea of faces that know what it is like to be manipulated. We too know what it is like to be used. We have felt anger and have taken the poison ourselves. We must begin to model authenticity and invite young people into a "for giving" life. The greatest healing our culture needs is the liberating power of forgiveness—and especially the liberation from righteous indignation. Who is our Peggy today? Who, within our reach, is on the cusp of saying: "I want to live like that. I want to live authentically." Let's take Jesus there.

7 Advocates: The New Role for Youth Ministry

For this reason I remind you to rekindle the gift of God that is within you through the laying on of my hands, for God did not give us a spirit of cowardice, but rather a spirit of power and of love and of self-discipline. (2 Timothy 1:6–7)

H–E–L–P

A teacher at a nearby alternative school called me and said that one of her students had become listless and sullen. She asked if he wanted to see me (we had connected both in juvey and in our gardening outreach). His grades were dropping, his attendance was suffering, and she thought he might be slipping back into drugs. When I showed up at the school, Marcus was sitting alone in a classroom, looking down at the desk in front of him. As I entered, he raised his eyes for a second and then again, slowly lowered them. Mumbling, he said, "The teacher told you to come here, didn't she?"

I said: "Marcus, that doesn't matter. I would have come anyway if I thought you wanted to talk. But, since you mentioned it, she did say you might want to see me."

I knew enough about Marcus's home situation to know that it wasn't healthy, I also knew that Marcus, like so many young people, would feel like he was betraying his family if he opened the curtains to let me peer in. Marcus was sitting under a poster from the movie *Castaway* (Twentieth Century Fox, 2000).

The poster depicted the scene where Tom Hanks is marking out the huge letters H–E–L–P by shuffling in the sand with his feet. It was obvious that the chance of his petition ever being seen or heard was slim to nil. "Marcus," I said, "look at that poster. Is that how you feel, like a castaway writing unseen words in the sand?"

It must have struck a harmonic note for him because Marcus's eyes welled up with tears and he somehow managed to whisper, "Yes."

Marcus's father was drinking again, and when he drank he became aggressive and hostile. Marcus told me about going home and having his father push him against a wall shouting, "Stand up and face me like a man!" When Marcus didn't stand up at attention, his father would just yell more and call him derogatory names. Marcus didn't want to fight back and had no place else he could run to—his mother was with a new boyfriend, and that man didn't want Marcus in their house. However, if Marcus ran away, his father would call the probation officer and Marcus would go back to juvey. Marcus would be arrested when, in fact, he was the victim—the victim of a father who emotionally abused him, the victim of a county that had no other place to send him, and the victim of a community that didn't want to get involved. Marcus wanted to finish school. He wanted to go to college. He had hopes and dreams, but he felt completely powerless in his current situation. He was a castaway.

By working together with Marcus's teacher and probation officer, and by intervening with the father, we were able to ease the immediate stresses of the situation, but I can't help but think of all the young people like Marcus who do not have advocates. How many of them also feel like castaways, writing huge letters on lost beaches that will never be seen? H–E–L–P.

Ripe for Manipulation

This last week I spoke at a child abuse council about mentoring outreaches. Prior to my talk, the chief of police shared a map of the city with red spots on the areas where child abuse had been reported and yellow spots on the places where abuse had been verified during the previous month. The president of the council looked at the map, drew a deep breath and said, "It looks like our city has the chicken pox."

Our cities do have the pox. Our youth are far less safe than the adults in our community, and the gap seems to be widening.

Young people are at the front line of the pox in our cities, and it is obvious that they know who around them is being violated long before we do as adults. Yet they live behind a veil of silence. They exist on deserted islands like castaways, crying for H–E–L–P but hopelessly watching as the tide comes in and washes away the letters even as they write them. Young people need to know how to be aware of and deal with violence and its ugly root: manipulation. They need to know how to safely and confidentially support others and how to get help in extremely high-risk situations. But more than anything, young people need advocates.

In Marcus's case, we got him out of the home for a respite. Then together, Marcus, his probation officer, and I worked out a short-term strategy on how Marcus should physically and emotionally respond when his dad was angry: "Don't be defiant or stare angrily into his eyes. Instead, tell your dad, 'Dad, I really love you, but I don't know what to do when you are so angry at me.'" If that does not de-escalate the situation, his probation officer told Marcus that he had permission to immediately leave, go to a friend's house, and call for help. We then rehearsed the strategy multiple times, role-playing the situation so Marcus's response would be immediate. We shared the strategy with Marcus's father so that he knew we were aware of Marcus's plight and attuned to his cry for help. We didn't want Marcus to ever have to "man up" to his father again.

Many young people, like Marcus, wind up in detention, not because they are unsafe to the community, but because the community is unsafe for them and our counties have no other place for them to go. In fact, I would say that most young people I have met who were incarcerated or expelled fit this category. Their lives are lose-lose propositions. Their cries of H–E–L–P have been washing out to sea for years. They are the "blamed victims" of our system.

But we cannot look at the statistics and say, "Those are just troubled kids." Even if our kids are not coming from violent homes, their risk of being victims is in direct proportion to their vulnerability, and their vulnerability compounds when they are cloaked in a veil of silence. Blaming the victim is a sin of omission that exacerbates the violence by ignoring the cause. Lack of advocacy is not the cause, but it is one of the most prevalent reasons our young people are such prime targets. In my programs, the level of emotional and physical abuse decreases when a mentor meets with the youth, the parent, and the probation officer right at the get-go. We have even noticed a change in the harshness of sentencing when a mentor appears in court with a young person. One judge told me it is because he can see that the youth has at least one firm lifeline in his or her life, and, he says, "One is often all it takes." That same judge told me that he would rather do anything than incarcerate a youth, but so few advocates for these alienated young people are in our community. Youth advocacy is the fastest growing need for youth ministry in the United States, and we must be at the forefront. We can change the scope of our communities if we just see our role as "connecting young people to community and connecting communities to young people."

Blaming the Victim

Is blaming the victim a new trend in our world? Not hardly. We can again turn to the Gospels and see how Jesus handled victim-blaming in the political and religious pressure cooker of Jerusalem. Seeking to discredit Jesus, the religious leaders (in this case the scribes who were like religious attorneys) throw before him a woman who had been caught in adultery (see John 8:3–11). If she had actually been caught in adultery, one has to wonder why the man wasn't caught as well. The woman is obviously not brought before Jesus for her sin as much as for the religious leader's political agenda. Those leaders knew that Jesus embraced sinners, but would he embrace this sinner? After all, she was an adulteress! If he forgives her, the leaders can say he is against Mosaic Law, and therefore he is no prophet. If he condemns her, he must take her to the edge of town and pick up the first stone to kill her. Just what is Jesus's response to this apparent setup?

The woman has sinned, but she is obviously a victim of a larger ploy over which she has no control. The religious authorities use this woman as a tool to discredit Christ. It is their injustice that is really on trial here. It is their calloused treatment of the poor and destitute that is really being called into question. They want to rid themselves of the truth (Jesus) so they can continue to live in systemic sin, so they can continue to blame the victim. They are trying to reduce Jesus to their level of self-righteousness, prejudice, and legal adherence. They hate love but love judgment—that's the bottom line.

The adultress stands there defenseless, absolutely vulnerable, completely and utterly exposed—many of our youth today can completely identify with her feelings—but Jesus stands up for her. He becomes her advocate. He sees every smirking smile and every sweaty fist touting the jagged stone of judgment in the crowd, and yet he is completely ambivalent toward them. He has no fear, no need for personal justification. He kneels down and writes in the sand. Notice that our Lord doesn't say, "Let any among you who have committed adultery throw the first stone at her." Nor, does he say, "Let any among you who have committed an equally grievous sin . . ." No, our Lord states, "Let anyone among you who is without sin be the first to throw a stone at her" (John 8:7).

"Without sin." "Without any sin."

Jesus doesn't condone her sin, but he doesn't condemn her either—even though he alone had the right to cast that first stone. Our commission lies in recognizing our visceral attachment to these victims—like this woman and like Marcus—and then advocating for those victims in the same manner that Jesus advocated for this woman. Instead of blaming the victims, we are to clench them tightly into our arms, free them from their bonds, and disarm the crowd.

"Woman, where are they? Has no one condemned you?" She said, "No one, sir." And Jesus said, "Neither do I condemn you. Go your way, and from now on do not sin again." (John 8:10–11)

Here is another aspect of the beloved blessing that elaborates upon the rest:

- "This is my Son, the Beloved, with whom I am well pleased."
- "You know everything I did and you still love me."
- "They know what I was, but now look at who Jesus made me."
- "I was a victim—and Jesus stood up for me."

We are called to respond and break through the silence in the same manner as Jesus. One hand embraces the violated, the other disarms the crowd. Dr. Martin Luther King Jr., conveyed this commission when, on July 30, 1966, in the New Friendship Baptist Church in Chicago, Illinois, he stood before a crowd and stated: "We are aware that the existence of injustice in society is the existence of violence, latent violence. We feel we must constantly expose this evil, even if it brings violence upon us" (Oates, *Let the Trumpet Sound,* p. 397).

It is a cultural sin to look the other way, to blame the victim. Negligence is a sin of omission. We hide behind the illusion of powerlessness: "What can one person do anyway?" Yet it is a Gospel imperative to find the victims in our community and force the crowds around them to disarm. We need to do as Jesus commanded "'Go therefore into the main streets, and invite everyone you find to the wedding banquet'" (Matthew 22:9). We don't need a new program to do this—we don't need a committee to study it (it isn't "for God so loved the world . . . he sent a committee"). What we need is one adult who cares enough to sit down with one youth, period. One at a time, that's all we need. But it begins with modeling. We must be the first models of advocates to our community.

This is Christ-centered leadership, to go out into the pool and tell people, "Come on in, the water is great." Authentic leaders would never stand on the deck and tell others to jump in. Authentic leaders would never send people to do what they would not do personally.

Can you imagine the impact a whole church would have if it were invited to pursue just such a task? Can you imagine teams of six or seven families focusing on one neighborhood that had one or more red and yellow pox dots? It would fulfill the prophecy of Isaiah that told us that Jesus would delight to go to the castaways, to the islands of despair and bring them great news!

> Here is my servant, whom I uphold,
>   my chosen, in whom my soul delights;
> I have put my spirit upon him;
>   he will bring forth justice to the nations.
> He will not cry or lift up his voice,
>   or make it heard in the street;
> a bruised reed he will not break,
>   and a dimly burning wick he will not quench;
>   he will faithfully bring forth justice.
> He will not grow faint or be crushed
>   until he has established justice in the earth;
>   and the coastlands wait for his teaching.
>
> (Isaiah 42:1–4)

The word for *coastlands* is also the word for *islands*. It is where the disheartened wait, fainting and crushed, for the sound of justice to ring. That is where the Lord sends us—to the castaways, the youthful victims who are blamed for their victimhood. Let us break the veil of silence and run to the islands. Let us go forth to bring justice to all nations and all islands.

The Least Engaged

Who has the most power in any relationship? Isn't it the one who is least involved?

For example, if a husband is not involved in a marriage, the other members of that family are victims of his disengagement. They often will do anything to keep him involved, tiptoeing around his mood swings as if there were a rattlesnake loose in the house and everyone jumped when they heard it. If a teenager is not involved in a family, the whole family—not just the teen—is "at risk" by his or her disengagement. If a young person is not engaged in a classroom, then that one individual quickly becomes the center of attention. Until that youth is engaged, the teacher will have to expend all of his or her energy trying to control that student, often at the expense of the other students. If the rules of a society exclude a class of people very long, that society will eventually be taken hostage or terrorized by those who have the least to lose in the current system. Our questions—the questions of Christ-centered leadership—must always be, "Who has the least to lose in my relationships? Who is the least engaged in my community? in my church? in our nation? in our world?"

The role of a Christian leader is to find the disengaged and build bridges to them. Please note the inference: It is not good enough to be missionaries to our youth (as many youth ministers are); it is imperative that we build bridges between our young people and the mainstream community. They need to become engaged in the community! Our youth need adults, and our adults need our youth. Our job is to create bridges that they both can cross into meaningful community! We need to "connect young people to community and communities to young people."

Christ compares us to the leaven or yeast in bread (see Matthew 13:33 and Luke 13:21). The leaven is the change-agent, it takes so little leaven to change the whole structure of the bread. We in ministry must be change-agents in our communities. Ideally, if we do it right, people will not even know we exist. The apex of Christ-centered success is when an alienated group of people feels like *they* made the change—or as Christ would tell so many people, "Your faith has healed you." We become the agent of change from the inside out, and the only sign that we were ever present is that our communities are fuller and richer than before we arrived. We absolutely can change the structure of power within our communities by engaging the disengaged, by bringing justice to the islands, by standing up for the sinner, by advocating for Marcus.

The Prophetic Role

We literally change the face of our community when we provide meaningful involvement to the least involved young people. When I change the life of one gang-involved youth, that young person can do more to change my community then I will ever be able to accomplish even if I talk to all the churches and service groups in my town! These are the ways we can teach young people to not be victims, to be less susceptible to manipulation, even to become known as peacemakers in the midst of trouble. In fact, the more we teach youth to be peacemakers, the less likely they are to act out in violent ways.

Communities that are openly and honestly dealing with the issues of violence and abandonment recognize the need for seeking out the negative kids and getting them involved early.

What is our role as leaders for Christ and advocates of youth? Our role is not to point fingers and blame the community for their lack of foresight; rather, our role is to bridge the gap. We often think that being prophetic is pointing out social and religious problems, but being prophetic is more than cynicism; it is pointing out social and religious solutions. Our prophetic role in youth ministry must be to create opportunities for adults and youth to connect in healthy relationships. It is what Jesus did for the woman caught in adultery. He embraced the sinner and disarmed the crowd. This is advocacy at its prophetic core. This is our Gospel call. Can you imagine being a church in which alienated youth in your community say (like the woman caught in adultery), "I was a victim, and those people stood up for me."

Last night in juvey, I closed the session with a prophetic challenge to the young people: "Whom do you know who is helpless, and how can you make them feel valuable?" They did not give complicated lists of new programs to start. They simply said: "I can play soccer with the little kid across the street. He is only eleven, and his whole family is a bunch of druggies." "I can listen to my friend who ran away last week and is really hurting. She has nowhere to go and she is afraid of being locked up." "I can talk to my friend about seeing a counselor. I know she is being abused and needs help." "I just need to spend some more time with my little brother. No one really talks to him."

It's the little things these young people want—like leaven in the bread. I wish I could print up those responses and pass them along to every adult in my community: "This is what youth are asking of us. This is what teens in the detention center say would keep them out of trouble: Play soccer with me, listen to me, talk with me, . . . just spend time with me."

Advocates: The New Role for Youth Ministry

In my outreach ministry, I see that the primary problem facing young people is a lack of meaning and a sense of victimhood, being unable to do anything healthy about their situation. Repeatedly I have seen that by strengthening a young person's sense of meaning and value, I can make her or him less amenable to manipulation and less poised to being violated. Young people live in a vacuum of "spiritual list-lessness," a void formed by a culture that doesn't value values. Many young people are not "getting" religion because they have never experienced spirituality as a viable source of empowerment in their lives. We have the challenge before us to respond by simply "loving like Jesus loved," without religious connotations or conditions. Isn't it enough that they will know we are disciples by our love (see John 13:35)? You and I have the opportunity to *evangelize* (a word which literally means "angels in the streets") in the custom attributed to Saint Francis of Assisi: "Teach the Gospel at all times; if necessary use words."

The longer we know young people, the more likely it is that they will ask, "Why do you even love me?" They are stunned by our compassion, at times literally confused by it. They test us for sincerity, authenticity. Yet we wait for the ripe moment to share our faith. When a child asks the question, "Why do you even love me?" that is the point in time I believe we have earned the right to respond simply and openly, "Because I've been a victim too and someone (Jesus) stood up for me." That is our modality for teaching a cognitive pathway to faith: "When someone has been my advocate, I want to become an advocate as well."

Will our youth know Jesus because someone advocated for them?

Most of the volunteers I work with are laypeople who say: "I don't know a lot about religion. I don't know much about the Bible. I am not equipped to preach." We say: "That's okay. Most people you will work with have a distrust of religion, have been beaten with bibles, and are not equipped to listen to sermons. But will you love them? Will you listen to them? Will you stand beside them as they open up their hearts and show you their fears?"

Give me someone who has compassion for young people, and in five minutes or less I can make him or her a great mentor for outreach programs. That should be the primary basis for participating in volunteer and ministry programs: "Do you have compassion for young people? Techniques and curriculum come a distant second, but do you care about kids?"

Our goal must be to "love like Jesus loved," to bless like God blessed, to give value to victims, to the violated and castaways in our communities.

We love like Christ loved when we don't insist that a person has to be like we are to be valuable. So, the greatest show of love in a life that is outcast is not our words but our presence, our unconditional consistency. It is when we show up no matter what they have done. Do you see Jesus's unconditional consistency in the story of the adulteress woman? Even in her grievous sin and in front of witnesses trying to entrap him, Jesus stands up for her. Can we stand up for Marcus even if he never shows up for Confirmation or Communion? Can we advocate for him even if he doesn't accept our doctrine or denomination? Are we willing to let go of our conditions and to love him like Jesus did?

The other day, the director of our juvenile center (whom I have worked with extensively for years) talked to me about other outreaches that have come in and tried to "convert kids." He said they never seem to follow up after the young people have "accepted Jesus Christ as their personal Lord and Savior." He said: "Your people realize that the last thing these kids need is another ideology. They just need to be loved unconditionally." I was humbled by that assessment of our work. For years, my cry has been, "Can't we just love them like Jesus would?"

If loving like Jesus loved means we are watering down the Gospel, then so be it. Let us be bold in our guilt. Yet, let us continue to advocate for loving young people sans conditions. The greatest statement we make to young people is to spend time with them. To come to them especially when they have been most inconsistent and, at that time, be least judgmental. It is at that time that our authenticity preaches louder than any words we could say. If they feel loved by us—believe me—they will want to know more about our source of strength.

When we give someone our time, we give them our most valuable commodity. And, youth, especially, perceive receiving attention as being valued. In fact, they will take any attention even if it is for errant behavior. The best way to teach young people that they are valuable and meaningful is to offer them uninterrupted attention. By that simple yet powerful act, we are showing young people that it isn't what they can do for us that matters. What matters is their inalienable right to unconditional love. We can translate that right into one question: "Who among the youth in your community has had the least amount of positive attention this week, and how do you build a bridge between your church and them?"

Imagine your church becoming the bridge that helps adults love kids where they are instead of saying, "You must come to where I am first." Imagine being on a rescue mission that finds adrift castaways and welcomes them with the simple message: "Hey, I know what it is like to feel completely alone and afraid. I was a victim too and someone stood up for me."

If young people feel valued and meaningful, then their ability to articulate what is meaningful and valuable in life will naturally flow from those relationships. Their cognition will follow their pathway, and their values won't be centered in things. They won't see people as tools to be manipulated or violated so they can get what they want. Instead, advocating for other people will hold a significant value to them and make their lives meaningful. That is radical change, root change; that is conversion!

I need to share something spectacular with you. I began working on this chapter two weeks ago and talked to the young people in juvey about the subject matter. I asked one of the youth (who has been frequently in juvey the last two years) to share about Holocaust survivor Viktor Frankl and his book *Man's Search for Meaning* (Boston: Beacon Press, 1959). He had been reading it with his mentor (now they are reading the plays of Shakespeare together). Our young friend said that Frankl can best be summarized in these words: "If you have a 'why' you can endure any 'way.'"

In the middle of the session, the young man's probation officer came in and took him aside to tell him that he was going to be sentenced to a long-term youth detention facility on the other side of the state for at least eighteen months. He would stay behind bars until he was eighteen years old so that he didn't have to return to his home. This young man was actually excited. You see, he is another young victim to whom "home equals hurt." Though his father is abusive, the courts have continued to send him home as the best of available alternatives. Bob (the young man) endures his home as long as he is able, but it is a hopeless, no-win situation to him. So, in response, he continually runs away. He hangs out with street friends on the run until he gets caught and winds up in juvey again. This last time he pleaded with the courts to sentence him until he was no longer a juvenile and didn't have to go home anymore. He told his mentor and me: "This is more of a home to me than my home. Nobody tries to beat me up here. I eat regular meals. I am safer here than there."

He then asked to talk to the whole group about his situation and told them: "I have a why. I can take this way." Then, paraphrasing Frankl once again, he said: "The last liberty is choice, choice of attitude. I can choose to grow no matter what my circumstances."

It is a horrible commentary on our "omission society" when the safest place for some young people is behind bars. Yet, it is an even graver sin to see the enthusiasm and desire for meaning among youth stifled just when it is at its peak. Can we move our churches and communities beyond blaming the victims to embracing them? Can we give them meaning by seeing their value? Isn't the apathy and listlessness that so many adults accuse youth of displaying more their curse than their fault? We can change that if we give young people a "why" to endure their "ways." We can engage the disengaged and give them purpose. We can be advocates, and we can be prophets for a new generation. We can "connect young people to communities and communities to young people." Indeed we must.

8 Freedom from Dependency

"Come to me, all you that are weary and are carrying heavy burdens, and I will give you rest. Take my yoke upon you, and learn from me, for I am gentle and humble in heart, and you will find rest for your souls. For my yoke is easy, and my burden is light." (Matthew 11:28–30)

Find Help!

Larry and Maureen Reynold have been retired for about ten years. For the last two, they have been faithful mentors in the local juvenile outreach programs in my community. They have gone to court with young people and visited them when they were sent to institutions far away from town. They planted seeds with young people in our garden and bought vegetables when those seeds grew ripe and firm. Their energy and enthusiasm never ceases to amaze me, and I wish I could clone them fifty times over.

In one mentoring session, I asked the young people to identify people whom they admire, locally or globally. Then, I asked them to contact those people and (1) tell them of their admiration; and (2) ask those heroes about what influences helped them build their character.

The Reynolds were working with Eduardo, who talked about his admiration for an author named Luis Rodriguez. Mr. Rodriguez wrote a book called *Always Running: La Vida Loca, Gang Days in Los Angeles* (Carmichael, CA: Touchstone Books, 1994).

"But," said Eduardo, "there's no way he would talk to me." I told Eduardo that no one in the world is more than four or five relationships away from us; we just need to work on the right networks to reach them. Most of the young people laughed and said, "Yeah, . . . right."

However, Larry and Maureen took "Yeah, . . . right," as a personal challenge. They worked with Eduardo during the session to draft a letter to Mr. Rodriguez, asking what inspired him to get out of the gang lifestyle. This wonderful retired couple took the letter home and e-mailed the author's publisher. Within an hour, Mr. Rodriguez had responded with a five-point plan on how he was able to leave behind *la vida loca* (the crazy life).

Mr. and Mrs. Reynold called me immediately and asked if they should wait until the next session to take that letter in to show Eduardo. "Of course not!" I replied. So they took the letter to Eduardo's class immediately. The teacher of the alternative program had Eduardo read it out loud to all the students.

The Reynolds took a huge step in building Eduardo's maturity on the day they sent his letter to Mr. Rodriguez. It is critical that we help young people identify friends outside their immediate circles who can expand their lives in healthy ways.

All of us know there is a great deal of truth to the statement, "It's not what you know but who you know." Young people need to learn that who you know doesn't have to be an accident of fate. They can choose to expand their friendships in a manner that will exponentially change their world. What was it those students in Eduardo's class learned more than anything else? None of us is bound by the circumstantial relationships of our life; instead we can reach out and make purposeful relationships—far beyond our own circumstances. Mr. Rodriguez put it much more simply in his letter to Eduardo: "Find help."

Dependency Cycles and Manipulation

About fifteen years ago, I began to use some various terms to describe what I was witnessing in adolescent behavior and the emotional development (or arrest) of incarcerated young people. I witnessed four stages of dependency that greatly impacted the ability of the young people with whom I was working to attain and sustain maturity. I agree with Erik Erikson's psychosocial development theories in that I do not believe we always pass from one stage to another. We can, in fact, become arrested in any of the stages if our development is frozen because of a crisis, such as compulsive behavior, addictions, abuse, or, as I stated in the last chapter, self-righteousness.

Stage One: Dependence

In the dependence stage, young people are completely dependent on a significant other for their esteem. They feel esteemed when their needs are met on a consistent basis. To the degree that young people learn that their actions can lead to consistent reactions in the world around them, they begin to see order in their lives. That sense of "action causes orderly reaction" will eventually color their whole viewpoint of life, including whether they see the world as a hostile place where they are a victim or an orderly place over which they have some proactive control. It is also in this stage that the seeds are laid for their ability to view God as a loving creator or whether they have a deep conviction that life is chaos and God is either nonexistent or, at best, indifferent to them.

If young people feel like they can take some control over their environment, they want to grow. They want to see just how much control they can take. This is necessary to move into the next stage of development—anti-dependence.

My visits to jails have led me to believe that most incarcerated females are arrested in a dependency stage. They would do anything to keep the approval of their significant other, which makes them horribly easy to manipulate. A young person stuck in the dependency cycle may go as far as selling drugs, fighting, lying, and even selling her or his own body to keep or gain the approval of their significant other. I witness this so frequently in the young females that I see who feel stuck in the system. All too often there is a manipulative other in the background that keeps a young girl dangling by that need for approval and, as we have said before, one of our biggest hurdles in life is to be liberated from craving the approval of the person who is least likely to give it to us.

We can assist young people to move beyond the stage of dependence by teaching them the vital difference between approval and authentic love. We can teach dependent young people that living to be accepted is a setup. It is critical for those we love to know that manipulative others will only increase their demands the more the dependent person tries to please them. We liberate the dependent young person when we invite him or her into an authentic love and introduce him or her to the author of authenticity: Jesus Christ himself.

Stage Two: Anti-Dependency

If young people learn that they can actually influence the world around them, then they will assertively (and sometimes very assertively) try to break away from what makes them feel dependent. Some call the initial onset of this struggle the "terrible twos," others call it "counter-dependence" or "oppositional behavior." In truth, the anti-dependent child is not being terrible—she or he is just asking, "Exactly how much control do I have over my own world?"

Normally this stage begins when a child realizes he or she is a separate entity from the parent. The child discovers his or her fingers, toes, crawling, walking, and . . . the child discovers his or her voice. Once that happens, it doesn't take the child long to discover the one-word sentence every parent seems to fear, "No!"

The advances in neuroscience, and particularly its emphasis on adolescent cognitive pathways, tell us that youth are also literally rediscovering their body and brain connection again at pubescence. It is a second individuation process that can last well into the late teens. Teenagers have learned to say "No," but now they are learning to say, "No way!" That's more than twice the vocabulary they had when they were in their terrible twos! One mother told me that "raising an adolescent today is like being bitten to death by ducks." Welcome to the adolescent version of anti-dependence.

If, during this stage, teens learn that it is okay to openly, but respectfully, express themselves, if they have a caring adult who allows them the appropriate latitude to make their own decisions, then, eventually, they begin to tire of the anti-dependent phase, and they are ready to move on. However, if they don't have that latitude to learn from their mistakes then they become stuck again.

Sadly, this is where I find most of the male inmates and detained youth with whom I work. They are stuck in anti-dependence, being defiant and hostile toward anyone who so much as stares at them. I can't count how many gang members have told me, "He was mad dogging (staring at) me, so I had to hit him!" I would ask, "Did he learn his lesson?" "Oh yeah, man," I hear. "I really put him down."

"Wow," I respond. "So, where is he now?" "I don't know, probably back in the neighborhood." "And," so I ask, "you are . . . where?" If the moment is right, I can say: "It doesn't seem like this behavior is working toward your advantage. How many times have I seen you in here now? Are you ready to try something else?"

Young people are freed when they witness healthy models of authentic adulthood. Teens desire to move beyond arrested development when they encounter and are blessed by people who choose a life of compassionate service and, through compassion, include them in their lives. Young people are freed when they can finally say: "I am tired of coming back inside these same walls and winding up with the same results. Help me!"

The young person who wants better solutions, who seeks something better than the anti-dependent life, will look for something more than just repeatedly saying, "No way!" That young person begins to ask, "What way works?" She or he enters a period of reflection and introspection that can last for days or years. I hear it all the time at crisis points from anti-dependent people, ages twelve to ninety-two: "There has got to be a better way than this."

Stage Three: Independence

I believe there is a searching stage when we actively look for alternatives somewhere beyond dependency and beyond anti-dependency. This is the stage of independence. Independence is a temporary stage where a young person takes stock of the way he or she has responded to life in the past and asks, "What works and what doesn't?"

In this stage young people are reflecting on what values will work for them and are examining what they have learned, looking at alternative responses to life, and beginning to think critically about what behaviors they will keep and what behaviors they will throw away. It is a very healthy stage of searching for "life ideals." It is a perfect stage for young people to be in mission and service and not just in a classroom.

A young person who successfully progresses through anti-dependence begins to establish her or his own sense of self, values, and friendships. The number of relationships diminishes in their lives, but the depth of their friendships deepens and their choice of friends is generally based upon a new-found (or at least newly named) sense of values. The young person is beginning to ask not only, "What am I going to be?" but on a deeper level, "Who am I going to be?" And even, "Who am I going to be with?"

To be present as a young person embraces the value of Gospel service and Gospel authenticity is perhaps one of the most exciting aspects of ministry. Watching a young person embrace service as a personal value is an indescribable blessing. There is a driving hunger during the time of independence to apply the values of the Gospel, to put them into practice. We simply must respond. We must give young people the opportunity to experience and try on their values in supportive communities and service-oriented outreaches. To not do this is a travesty. We would be missing one of the greatest windows of opportunity in our young people's lives.

This is what Jesus meant by planting the seed in deep soil so that its root can sustain it through droughts or storms. That crop will take deep root and change our world one community at a time. Will your church offer deep soil for the young seeds that Christ has given to us? Will young people focus outward with the lenses of Jesus or solely inward with the "my-optic" lenses of our culture? Will we provide opportunities to grow in service to the Lord who washed our feet? That is the type of action that helps young people move beyond dependence, beyond anti-dependence, even beyond independence, to the ultimate maturity of intra-dependence.

Stage Four: Intra-Dependence

Intra-dependence moves beyond independence when young people finally realize that it is healthy to be situationally dependent, anti-dependent, and independent. Young people are most mature when they can move freely through differing responses without being threatened or stuck in one particular stage. Young people may need to be dependent when they feel hurt or isolated. They may need to be anti-dependent when pressed to go against their values or when someone is trying to be manipulative. They may need to be independent when thinking through important life choices and needing either some time alone with God or with an accountability group.

Intra-dependence is the liberty to move from one repetitive response to all situations and instead be able to adjust our responses to the circumstances in which we find ourselves. Unhealthy people sticks with only one tool that they have used repeatedly (perhaps as early as infancy), and they use that same tool for every conflict throughout their entire lives. Maybe that tool is verbal bullying. Someone else's tool might be martyrdom, and they learn that if they go to pieces during stressful times, everyone will back off and leave them alone. Whatever the tool, the person gets attached to it, whether or not the result is optimal for continued growth.

This is like having only a hammer in your automobile's tool kit. Your car's air filter gets clogged, so you beat on it with a hammer. The result is that the car is dented and still doesn't work. You run out of fuel, so you get out a hammer and pound on the gas tank, but the car is dented, it still doesn't work, and maybe it even blows up. Then you say, "See, no matter what happens my car is always dented and it still doesn't work." Perhaps the most evident statement of being compulsively stuck in a stage is the statement, "No matter what I try, I always wind up in the same situation."

It is obvious that it is not the problem that needs fixing—it is the solution. The cyclical results that we often experience are not because our problems are always the same. It is because our solutions are always the same!

Intra-dependent young people are able to use the tools that work best for the problem at hand. As the problems around them change, they are not insecure about adapting and trying out new approaches. Change does not threaten them because at their core is an unshakeable sense of value and purpose.

Imagine growing intra-dependent young people. Imagine growing intra-dependent communities! This happens when young people have a sense of their beloved blessedness. They recognize that their core self is not up for sale or for grabs at any price. This is why Christ was not threatened in any situation. It is why Paul could face starvation, torture, and death without floundering. The blessing of God was at their core, a blessing no power in creation could manipulate:

> For I am convinced that neither death, nor life, nor angels, nor rulers, nor things present, nor things to come, nor powers, nor height, nor depth, nor anything else in all creation, will be able to separate us from the love of God in Christ Jesus our Lord. (Romans 8:38–39)

Maintaining the Intra-Dependent Life

When we are aware of these stages of dependency in our own lives, we will feel far less threatened as we assist others (especially the young people we serve) who might be stagnating in different stages of dependency. In fact, we can become healers by helping others recognize the competencies and challenges of progressing toward the intra-dependent life. We can help others focus on the ultimate goal, "Maturity is the ability to be who you need to be, when you need to be it."

God (who is ultimately the model of maturity, right?) gave himself this name: "I Am Who I Am" (Exodus 3:14).

For many young people, this might sound like the title of a rap song, but God is always who God needs to be, where God needs to be, and when God needs to be. Our Creator has a singular core value—assertively offering to restore us into divine relationship. That is literally God's delight! To be in relationship with "I Am Who I Am" is like standing in a crystal clear flowing mountain stream. God is able to touch upstream in our lives and change how we view the pain of our past. God is also is able to touch the rapids where we are standing, bringing us strength in the present. Finally, God will be there for us downstream before we ever arrive. What is more is that God can do all of this at once! Time and distance are irrelevant to God. They are just tools at our Creator's disposal.

Many poignant examples in the Scriptures indicate Jesus's ability to remain constant in an ever-changing environment, to be who he is no matter where he was. Jesus is the ultimate model of the intra-dependent person. Jesus exemplifies the kind of maturity that allows him the complete freedom to serve—to be a blessing—at any time, in any situation. Jesus was so comfortable with God's blessing that he didn't have to put on pretenses for anyone. Jesus was anti-dependent at times (toward Satan, the religious leaders, Pontius Pilate), he was independent at times (seeking God in prayer before every major decision of his life), and he was dependent at times (when he let Mary break her alabaster jar of perfumed ointment on his feet). He was mature in all situations (omniscient), he was able to respond appropriately and without compromise to his core values (omnipotent), and he was both servant and God (omnipresent) at all times.

What type of maturity do we seek for our young people? Isn't it the ability to live with the power of Christ, to authentically and maturely respond to all situations with the assurance of God's love. Can you imagine empowering youth to be dependent in times of great need, anti-dependent in the presence of the manipulative other, and independent as they seek out healthy responses based upon authentic values and compassion? If we offered them these gifts, they would indeed be manipulation-proof.

Legitimacy

Last night in juvey, I was called into a conversation with a fourteen-year-old Native American youth and asked him, "Abraham, what makes you legitimate?"

"I don't know," he responded.

"Do you have a younger brother or sister, Abraham?" (He had a younger brother). "Is he valuable to you?"

"Yes!" Abraham replied enthusiastically and talked about how he wanted to spend more time with his brother when he got out of juvey.

"What makes your brother valuable or legitimate?" I asked Abraham.

"Because I love him!" Abraham said with emphasis.

"Abraham, what makes you legitimate? What makes you valuable?" I asked.

Abraham looked down at the desk between us and rubbed his index finger in a slow, wide circle. I just waited patiently, expectantly. Then, sheepishly, without looking up, Abraham said, "Because you love me?"

"Abraham, there is no place in this world I would rather be than right here with you, right now. You hit the nail on the head. I do love you." (Talk about omniscient moments to offer the omnipotent power of God!)

"Abraham," I asked further, "do I love you because you are always good?"

"No," he responded.

"Do I love you because you are rich or have a 4.0 grade point average?"

"Maybe," he teased.

"Abraham," I leaned in. "Why do I love you?"

"Because I am valuable?" He looked up and smiled. "Because I'm . . . legitimate."

On his way out, Abraham went out of his way to stop by and talk with me again. He said: "I go to court tomorrow. I don't know what is going to happen. But whatever happens, I just want you to know that I think you are a really good person. I just didn't want to go without saying that to you."

Jesus said that the kingdom of God is like a mustard seed (see Matthew 13:31–32). It starts out as the smallest seed and becomes the biggest shrub in all of Judea. It is a really hardy plant that grows anywhere and doesn't require a lot of maintenance. In Christ's time, it was a poor man's gate because he could use it to fence off the house for safety and privacy. At the same time, it brought vibrant new life to the family because birds loved to lay their eggs in its thick branches. The mustard shrub provided safety, strength, and life to even the poorest of families. It was, as Jesus said, like heaven.

When we provide safety, strength, and life to the "least valuable" and "most outcast," we give them the opportunity to work through their dependency issues and become safety, strength, and life to others.

Any of us who have worked for a season with youth know what it looks like when a mustard seed takes root. It looks like Abraham saying, "I'm valuable." Give us the hardships, the mercurial highs and lows, take away the money and it sure ain't the prestige. But when one young person says, "I'm legitimate," well, the kingdom of heaven is like that.

The key word is *legitimacy*. But all too often I see young people bloodying their heads trying to go in the exit door. That's what it feels like when you are outside through no fault of your own. A friend and I go to court today with a young man named Stephen who has been in detention eighteen times since he was twelve. Most of the community would be only too eager to lock Stephen up and throw away the key. But they don't know what it is like to live with an abusive stepfather. They don't know what it is like to run away for fear of losing it when your mom is being beaten and the kids are forced to watch. His stepfather does the beating, but the young man goes to detention!

Long term, I plan on changing the system, but right now my task is to give honest legitimacy to this young outsider. In this case, I can't change the system in time to find Stephen a healthy home where he can be legitimately valued, but I can help him look to healthier places for legitimacy and authenticity. I can be there as the mustard seed takes root and well up with tears of joy when that seed grows up and says, "I am valuable."

The actions of so many of these young people are attempts at legitimacy. They are cries for approval and acceptance in a world where they cannot change a system in which they are forced to survive. I can't change the system by 1:30 p.m. today when the gavel cracks and the bailiff says, "All rise." But Stephen's mentor and I will be in court with him when he hobbles in with his shackles and orange jumpsuit. We will be there when he looks into the sparse crowd for a familiar face. He will see us and wave as best he can with hands cuffed behind his back, and he will know he is not alone. He will know he is legitimate, because like Abraham said, "You love me."

9 Motivating a New Generation of Visionaries

And I will ask the Father, and he will give you another Advocate, to be with you forever. This is the Spirit of truth, whom the world cannot receive, because it neither sees him nor knows him. You know him, because he abides with you, and he will be in you.

I will not leave you orphaned, I am coming to you. (John 14:16–18)

The Holy Motivator

The Holy Spirit was sent to comfort us, but the word *comfort* meant a far different thing to those persecuted during Jesus's last days and the early days of the Church than it might mean to us today. Compare our contemporary understanding of *comfort* with the Latin root *comfortis,* which means "to be with us in strength." The difference is that our definition of *comfort* seems to imply a peace without chaos while the Lord's definition is peace in the midst of chaos.

Similarly, the Greek term for Holy Spirit, *parakletos,* has connotations that may be in contrast to our culture. Scottish theologian William Barclay, cites these two major uses in his word studies on the New Testament:

> The word *parakletos* has a great background in Greek law. The parakletos was the prisoner's friend, the advocate and counsel for the defence, the man who bore witness to his friend's character when he most needed it, and when others wished to condemn him.

The word *parakalein* is the word for exhorting men to noble deeds and high thoughts, it is especially the word of courage before battle.

(Barclay, *New Testament Words*, p. 222)

Consider the implications of the terms *parakletos* and *parakalein* to the early Christian:

1. The Holy Spirit stands up for us and argues our case when we are most vulnerable.
2. The Holy Spirit is also our motivation, urging us to remain strong when we feel most afraid, to have courage when we are most alone, and to know peace when life is most chaotic.

We, in turn, bring the Holy Spirit to young people when we stand beside them while they are most rejected and encourage them when they are most unsure.

Motivating Youth to Pursue a Life-Encompassing Vision

In my work with incarcerated, recovering, or expelled kids, motivation takes the form of helping young people develop and name their own goals even while they are waiting to be adjudicated. A key component to my work with youth is a goal and task list and a weekly calendar. Each young person works with a mentor and together they examine seven areas of personal development: educational, financial, physical, professional, recreational, relational, and spiritual. Goal sheets have space for these seven major goals and then three lines for subtasks under each major goal. The role of each mentor is to help the young person identify his or her goals in each of the seven areas and then work toward creating measurable tasks that will bring the young person closer to his or her own vision of a meaningful life.

For example, Arturo was a fourteen-year-old who told me that his hero was Tony Hawk. Hawk was a professional skateboarder— now retired—but he has his own line of products and video games. I asked Arturo how much he thought Tony Hawk practiced every day when he was skating professionally, and Arturo said, "Probably for hours and hours."

"Arturo, what about you? Could you practice two hours, three days a week and still keep up with your homework?"

"Sure," said Arturo, "that's easy. I could do more than that."

"Well, let's start there," I said. "When could you do it?"

"Well, maybe Monday, Wednesday and Friday," Arturo said.

I asked Arturo, "If you got on a jet plane and the pilot said to you, 'Maybe I can fly you to L.A.' would you stay on the plane?"

Arturo smiled and jokingly said, "Maybe!"

"So, are you going to try to do this 'maybe' or are you going to do it?"

"I'm gonna do it." Arturo made this statement with absolutely resolve slamming his fist into his palm.

"Okay, let's write that on the calendar, then." I turned the sheet over to the calendar side. "Arturo, what's the most dangerous time of the day for you? The time you are most tempted to use drugs?"

"Usually right after school," Arturo responded.

"Okay, then let's write this task down from 3:00 p.m. to 5:00 p.m. Do you have any sober friends who like to skateboard and would show up to board with you?" I searched a little more.

"Yea, Jaime would do it." Arturo started to get really excited about his new plan.

"Good, when can you call Jaime and ask him to board with you?" I asked.

"I will try . . . er, I will call him as soon as I get out on Thursday," said Arturo.

"Great, Arturo! So, where do we write that down?" He penned it into the goal chart under "physical" and then wrote the date on his calendar as well.

"There," he said, "cool, huh?" He was proud to show me how fast he was catching on to the process.

Friends, can you see what Arturo and I were doing together? We were helping a young man achieve goals he set for himself. In the process, we took a drug dealer and major gang member off the streets during his most dangerous time. Arturo may or may not ever become a professional boarder, but the skills of planning will follow him throughout his life. When we met a week later, after his release, he proudly showed me the goals he had checked off and some additional goals he wanted to accomplish.

I had asked Arturo to do a little Internet research about Tony Hawk's background, and he learned that Mr. Hawk was an astute businessman. Suddenly, Arturo began to see a reason to study math and improve his reading skills. Arturo began to see education as a means to an end, and he set up a meeting with a tutor in math for the next week. His motivation switched from external to internal. He was ready to get moving. He was motivated!

Arturo is doing great today. He has an ongoing mentor whom he sees weekly to go over his goal and task sheet and weekly planner. He has increased his third-grade reading level significantly, and he has just successfully completed his probation agreement.

I find that one of the greatest joys in my life is to actually get young people sentenced to their own goals. I get to watch them as they proudly check off their weekly accomplishments. I get to see them begin to believe in themselves and their ability to achieve the goals that they set to deepen their lives. I ask them how it feels to accomplish their tasks, and when they have a hard week, I ask them what the roadblocks were, and then we strategize on how to get around them.

I especially love it when young people start mapping out their own spiritual and relational goals and I see them take an assertive part in identifying and pursuing eternal goals. Isn't that what we all long to witness? Isn't that the work of the Advocate (see John 14:16)? It is not that we do the work for those young people either; in fact, quite the opposite is true. We help them identify what they need to do in order to achieve the goals that are closest to their heart. We help them become fully human. We become paracletes to them, standing beside them, guarding their goals, and pushing them to seek the most out of life.

The Holy Spirit is the holy motivator who brings power, courage, and strength to our lives so that we can "bring good news to the poor" (Luke 4:18). That is the Holy Spirit we want our young people to embrace—living, vibrant, and real! We reveal the paraclete when we stand back-to-back or side-by-side with youth as they enthusiastically embrace life. We help them see an achievable road toward their own lifelong growth. We help set them free. We become holy motivators!

Motivational Force

Have you ever walked into a religious education class and seen young people with eyes glazed over and drool rolling out the sides of their lower lips? Did you, as a newbie, ever say, "How many of you want to learn about God?" only to have half the class look at you like you were a mouse that just tunneled up into the cat's basket? Let me share a similar experience.

If I walk into a detention center and say, "How many of you want to come back here again?" the answer is totally different than if I ask, "How many of you expect to come back here again?" There is obviously no desire among most of those young people to return to juvey, but there is a huge expectation that they will. The result is that many young people look at the odds ahead of them and feel like, "Why even try?"

How many youth in our church wonder the same thing? "What's the point?" "What has this got to do with real life?" In fact, if religion isn't tied to their relational experience, then there is no point to religion as far as the young people are concerned. We may consider faith the ultimate value, but our consideration is immaterial if it doesn't translate into a faith that is functional in their circumstances and viable in their daily experience. "What do these values have to do with my life?" "What value do they hold for me?" "I can practice them with you, but you're not always there. What do I do when it's just me, and my friends are pressuring me to forget my values?"

We cannot blame young people for asking these questions. They live in a culture whose modus operandi is "What's in it for me?" We need to make faith relevant to their experience and their needs. Faith has to be something they value, which, in essence, means it has to make them feel valuable.

Last week in detention, leaders from three different gangs were represented in the meeting room. I asked a question of the entire group, "How many of you have a little brother or sister in this community?"

The majority of participants raised their hands. "What would be your vision for their Walla Walla, the community in which they are going to grow up?"

By not focusing on their own needs, the young people agreed that they wanted a Walla Walla that was safe, emotionally and physically, for their little brothers and sisters. That was their optimal vision of their community. Of course, that led to the next questions: "Is what you are doing now going to lead toward that vision or away from it? How can you make the community safer for them?"

Suddenly, the room ignited with discussion on how we could make our town safer for the children on our streets. One young gang leader stopped the process and said, "Wait a minute, why do you think gangs are all bad?"

I said: "Did you hear me say that? Or, did you hear me say that gangs can have a positive or a negative influence? It completely depends on the leaders."

Caesar (the young man who asked the question) replied: "You can't just change a gang like that. If I told my people we were going to be 'peacemakers' they would laugh at me, then beat me up, then laugh at me some more."

I could see by his passion that Caesar desired the goal, but his expectancy of achieving that goal and the possibility of it being attainable were very negative. The result was a very passionate response that some might have interpreted as disrespectful. However, this type of behavior is truly indicative of exactly how much passion a person has for the topic.

"Caesar, what if you didn't tell anyone or seek anyone's approval? What if you just started practicing the principles of peacemaking and other people admired how you lived and wanted to become like you? You don't have to say anything . . . you just have to become a servant like César Chávez or Martin Luther King Jr."

Suddenly, Caesar saw a world of possibility. He came up to me immediately after the class and said, "I get out tomorrow. I am sick of coming back here. I'm too old for this game. Can you get someone to help me understand more about this leadership thing? I want to be like that. . . ."

By 8:30 the following morning, when I called juvey to set up a mentoring appointment for Caesar, he had already talked to his probation officer who was just about to call me. By the next day, Caesar was signing a mentoring agreement to pursue his own goals with his probation officer, his new mentor, and me.

From now on, the three of us will sit down with Caesar every week and help him deepen his goals. We need to let him tell us about his accomplishments and learn how we can advocate for him as he becomes a visionary in our community. To amplify his development, we can ask questions like, "Do you feel excited about what you accomplished this week?" That is far better than, "I feel proud of what you did." It lets him own his own progress.

When Caesar, Arturo, or any young person lacks motivation we tend to blame it on them, instead of looking deeper. We need to ask questions like the following:

- What do I need to change to motivate Caesar?
- What component am I not giving him?
- Is there value? "Does Caesar value this value? Would it impact his life in a tangible way?"
- Is there expectation? "Does Caesar believe this value is actually applicable in his circumstances? Does he really expect it to make a difference given his environment?"
- Is there application? "Does Caesar see the practicality of this value? Does he see how he could actually make it work effectively in his daily life? It may be an instrumental value to me, but is it instrumental to him?"

If just one component is missing or negative (a negative value), then the whole equation will become a negative to Caesar or Arturo or any young person who you see. Indeed, if they really want what you are offering to them but see no practical way to obtain it, they will actually attack the value—they will tune out or turn away. What we are trying to teach can turn against us. It is not the premise of faith that's rejected, it's the practice. That is our role as advocate leaders—to move faith from a concept to a lifestyle, from premise to practice.

Bring Them into the Vision

Last week, a principal for a Christian Recovery School came out to spend three days visiting the community youth outreaches in our county. At the end of the week, we sat down and she asked, "How can I apply what you guys are doing in this community to my school?"

She was there when we had the discussion with Caesar and the other gang-involved youth in juvey. I told her, "Bring the kids into your vision and help them go out and make it theirs."

I went on to say: "The most important question we asked last Tuesday was not 'What is your vision?' but instead, 'How many of you have a little brother or sister in this community?' That was the question that invited the young people into higher purpose. It was a vision that was important to them. They already believed it was valuable, they just never expressed it. Our role is to help them make it achievable!"

"The young people sent to you for discipline problems are the very kids that can change your school community. Those are the ones you can bring into the vision. Articulate the vision and write it on your board. Talk about it everywhere you go. Our goal is 'a safe place for all young people, emotionally and physically, a place where everyone can have a shot at reaching their greatest potential.'"

"Your job as a leader is to keep that vision alive, by telling its story. Publicly catch young people doing 'things right.' Could you imagine how fun your job would be if you got these young people to proclaim that vision?"

Let's all imagine that. Could you imagine if that were your full-time job? Could you imagine if your job description read: "Catch young people doing things right and brag about them." Imagine moving from disciplinarians or teaching young people something they are not motivated to learn to the joy of helping youth become vision bearers and holy motivators.

Creating Motivated Visionaries and Holy Motivators

Integrity, listening, empowerment, self-motivation, team development, cooperation—these are some of the critical traits required of leaders in today's world. They were identified by psychologist Daniel Goleman through years of studies and shared in his monumental book *Emotional Quotient* (New York: Bantam Books, 1995).

Goleman gives us wonderful news that all of these traits of leadership, which he refers to as the Emotional Quotient or EQ, can be learned and developed with practice. These critical characteristics are not genetically predisposed (determined prior to birth) like our Intelligence Quotient (IQ).

Dr. Goleman lists five primary goals in two areas of competency, which must be learned in order to achieve a life of purpose and meaning.

Personal Competence.

The following goals determine how we manage ourselves:

- Self-awareness or knowing one's internal states, preferences, resources, and intuitions.

- Self-regulation or managing one's internal states, impulses, and resources.
- Motivation or the emotional tendencies that guide or facilitate reaching goals.

Relational Competence.

The following goals determine how we handle relationships:

- Empathy or an awareness of others' feelings, needs, and concerns.
- Social skills or an adeptness at inducing desirable responses in others.

(Goleman, *Working with Emotional Intelligence,* pp. 26–27)

A high EQ translates into the ability to initiate change, develop collaboration, and create a sense of team. A person with a high emotional quotient is also adept at forming relationships with key people who will be instrumental in sharing and achieving established goals. Remember that is what we have defined as basic to becoming a healthy adult.

When I was in college, most studies of success evaluated only a person's position and financial wealth as primary indicators of success. They focused on issues like a need for control, power, and achievement. The more I read, the more I realized that what our culture was calling successful was equivalent to what a doctor would cite as a prime heart-attack candidate with a lousy family and communal life.

Think of the implications of Goleman's study for your work with young people and your church's involvement in the lives of young people in your community. In many situations religion has not been offered in a manner that shows a tangible or pertinent application in their lives. Much of our religious education is designed around public education models. We just trade one curriculum for another, but the emphasis is still on memory, not meaning. It isn't the curriculum that will help young people feel valued or assist them in valuing their faith.

Let's just recap for a moment what have we learned in the last few chapters:

1. Our goal is to help youth become God's blessing to others, no matter what their circumstances.

2. We believe that a healthy young person can state what she or he values and make life choices, including choosing key friendships based upon her or his values.
3. We know that young people learn about values through those who value them.
4. We understand that young people first practice their values and then name them.
5. We know that we are motivated only when we value a goal and have a sense of competence and achievability regarding that goal.
6. We know that learning how to self-motivate, communicate, and build community around our goals is the primary trait of a healthy adult or leader.

Do those six traits serve as a measuring stick for your ministry with youth? If we want to pass on important values, if we want to see young people have a viable and living faith, then we should measure every endeavor or curriculum against these six points.

Just yesterday, someone asked if they could give me a functioning Model-T Ford in good condition. I was elated! I had three choices:

• Fix it up and join a car club so I can show it off around the area.
• Fix it up and sell it on eBay and take a trip to Disney World with my family.
• Create a youth outreach that will utilize adults in my community to work alongside estranged youth. Let them work on the car together and enter it in car shows around the area. Our local youth center also just bought three ice cream carts for youth to make money to pay their fines and to have some spending money. At least one cart could go with the team to the car shows, raising awareness of the youth's vision, building more relationships, and increasing the chance of success for their microenterprise.

Let's use the six tools to evaluate my choices. Obviously, I would have to do a lot of rationalizing to make choice one or two fit the six-scale grid. However, the third option hits every button on the six-point scale.

1. Will young people feel like they are blessing themselves and others? Yes!
2. Will this program help young people identify some key adult values, like responsibility and teamwork? Yes!
3. Will this program help young people feel valued? Yes!

4. Will the young people be able to actually practice their values and then name what they are doing? Yes!
5. Will those motivated to participate in this program be able to develop the competency to do the project, and is there a high probability of success? Yes!
6. Will this program require self-motivation, teamwork, and community building? Yes!

   Dang . . . there goes Disney World again.

My friends, let's become holy motivators. Let's focus on raising young people who will be able to identify their values and build commitment around their goals. Maybe it won't get us to Disney World, but I think it will help us get a taste of heaven that is real and alive in the eyes of young people who "capture the vision."

Our Lord was fond of saying, "The kingdom is like . . ." Well, here's a thought, The kingdom of heaven is like the greasy, oil-covered face of a youth who smiles over his or her accomplishments and says, "If I can do that . . . I can do anything."

That's holy motivation.

10 Connecting Young People to Community and Communities to Young People

One thing I asked of the LORD,
  that will I seek after:
to live in the house of the LORD
  all the days of my life,
to behold the beauty of the LORD,
  and to inquire in his temple.

(Psalm 27:4)

Church: The House of the Lord

"To live in the house of the Lord" meant something distinct to the Hebrew culture. It was similar to saying, "I belong to the house of Jacob," which would mean, "I am part of Jacob's family, and he is my father (grandfather, great-grandfather)." To be in Jacob's house was to be a part of his clan and under his protection. Similarly, to be in the "house of the Lord" also means being part of God's family and under the protection of our Heavenly Ruler. The word that the Hebrews used for the people was *bayith* and the fullest definition of the term would translate into something like this: "a family where even my most vulnerable child could be raised in the safety and knowledge of God."

Here was the mission of all God's leaders: Abraham, Moses, Joshua, and Jacob, Sarah, Miriam, Ruth, and Esther; and the list pans out through the New Testament and down through the ages to contemporary leaders of God's house. To the extent that Martin

Luther King Jr., stood for the civil rights of all people, he stood for God's family. To the extent that Mother Teresa cared for the sick and dying who were Muslim, Christian, Hindu, or even atheist, she cared for God's family. All these leaders measured personal wealth by communal wholeness. Leadership was not how far an individual could get ahead, but a good leader was someone who used all of his or her resources to make sure no one would be left behind.

We are called not only to an advocate role to stand beside youth but also to a prophetic role to stand up for the youth in our communities. We are called to remind our communities about those it may be leaving behind in the pursuit of personal wealth or self-fulfillment. We are called to be prophets.

The prophetic role is ultimately not the role of government, the educational system, or social service agencies—it is our role. It is our role because we call ourselves followers of God, the God who tells us to "do justice, and to love kindness and to walk humbly with your God" (Micah 6:8). Christ is even more direct in Matthew 25:31–46 when he inflexibly tells us that if we do not know those who are alienated, incarcerated, or intimidated, then we do not know him. To know Jesus is to be "simple among the poor." We are to be both protector and advocate in the house of the Lord and that is the essence of "Church." To the extent that the Church does this work, it is building the house of the Lord, the *bayith* community. However, whenever we forget this duty (or allow our Church to forget it), we forget God's purpose, for we cannot be God's leader if we do not lead others toward God's purposes. God could not lay these purposes out any more clearly than he did when he pronounced his mission to the people of Nazareth:

> "The Spirit of the Lord is upon me,
> because he has anointed me
> to bring good news to the poor.
> He has sent me to proclaim release to the captives
> and recovery of sight to the blind,
> to let the oppressed go free,
> to proclaim the year of the Lord's favor."
>
> And he rolled up the scroll, gave it back to the attendant, and sat down. The eyes of all in the synagogue were fixed on him. Then he began to say to them, "Today this scripture has been fulfilled in your hearing." (Luke 4:18–21)

If that is Christ's mission statement and we are his followers, then that must also be our mission statement.

When the Son of Man comes in his glory, and all the angels with him, then he will sit on the throne of his glory. All the nations will be gathered before him, and he will separate people one from another as a shepherd separates the sheep from the goats, and he will put the sheep at his right hand and the goats at the left. Then the king will say to those at his right hand, "Come, you that are blessed by my Father, inherit the kingdom prepared for you from the foundation of the world, for I was hungry and you gave me food, I was thirsty and you gave me something to drink, I was a stranger and you welcomed me, I was naked and you gave me clothing, I was sick and you took care of me, I was in prison and you visited me." Then the righteous will answer him, "Lord, when was it that we saw you hungry and gave you food, or thirsty and gave you something to drink? And when was it that we saw you a stranger and welcomed you, or naked and gave you clothing? And when was it that we saw you sick or in prison and visited you?" And the king will answer them, "Truly I tell you, just as you did it to one of the least of these who are members of my family, you did it to me." Then he will say to those at his left hand, "You that are accursed, depart from me into the eternal fire prepared for the devil and his angels, for I was hungry and you gave me no food, I was thirsty and you gave me nothing to drink, I was a stranger and you did not welcome me, naked and you did not give me clothing, sick and in prison and you did not visit me." Then they also will answer, "Lord, when was it that we saw you hungry or thirsty or a stranger or naked or sick or in prison, and did not take care of you?" Then he will answer them, "Truly I tell you, just as you did not do it to one of the least of these, you did not do it to me." And these will go away into eternal punishment, but the righteous into eternal life. (Matthew 25:31–46)

Matthew tells us that we are closest to Christ when we are closest to his broken body present in this world. The further we get from the broken, the more we become like the Pharisees who had religion but lacked compassion (see Matthew 5:20). To the extent that the poor call us good news, we are living out the mission of Jesus Christ!

I mentioned in the previous chapter that I had been talking to the young people in juvenile detention about community leadership. When I asked them, "What kind of community do you want your little brothers and sisters to grow up in?" They responded with: (1) a community that is safe, emotionally and physically; and (2) a community where everyone has the opportunity to reach her or his fullest potential regardless of race, gender, or social class.

One young man in the group—Terry—has severe cerebral palsy. He raised his hand and struggled to get these words out: "I know what this means. Some people make fun of me because my body doesn't work. But this works (and he thumped his head with the back of his hand) and this works (and he thumped his heart in the same way). I just want the same chance that everyone else has."

When I sat with Terry yesterday, I asked him, "Whose potential could you unleash this week?"

In his labored words, he said, "Everybody here."

"Really, Terry? How could you do that?"

He said: "I can be an example. Yesterday, I mopped the floor of the whole detention center without being asked. I mopped the floor! I mopped the floor!"

That teenager, locked in one of our nation's thousands of detention centers, knows more about serving Jesus Christ than I have learned in decades of discipleship!

"I mopped the floor!"

My friends, here is the focus of the Christian life: Through Jesus Christ, we are to unlock the potential of everyone that we meet and unlock the potential of every community that we serve.

Like Terry, we are to be God's blessing no matter who we are, where we are, or what we have—even if all we can do is mop floors.

When Jesus saw the starving masses following him, he turned to his disciples and said, "You feed them." The disciples wanted to send the people away. There were thousands of them—an endless sea of hunger—and there was not enough food and not enough money to feed them. Yet, Jesus didn't see the impossibility of the situation; he saw the potential of God. He didn't look at his wallet and see how empty it was. He pulled out God's "Master Card" and charged it to the Creator. He literally turned and praised God for the potentiality of the situation—and the word Matthew uses . . . *eulogio!* Remember that word from the first chapter? It means to bless

God no matter what our circumstances are like, to take whatever is given to us and make it a gift to others.

While his disciples wanted to send the masses away, Jesus told them, "Bring them here to me" (Matthew 14:18). This is the heart of the Christian leader—to look at the needs of those around us and respond with, "Bring them here to me."

From Extended to Nuclear to the "Microwave Mob"

The majority of the world still lives with extended family. There, the responsibility for raising children does not fall upon a couple, an individual, or even a social institution (the increasing trend). It falls upon the entire village. Grandparents, uncles, aunts, cousins, and siblings are all included as part of the family of God.

Why did we switch from raising children in the healthy environment of an extended family to the failed experiment of the nuclear family?

The demise of the extended family was in direct proportion to the rise of the Industrial Age. We didn't move out of extended family situations because we began to hate our grandparents, uncles, and aunts. We transitioned because work was in the city and we couldn't take the extended family with us. Almost instantaneously we threw out the whole concept of extended family and became a nation of nuclear families.

The nuclear family was a failed experiment from the start, and it began to unravel quickly after its inception. It was highly dependent on strictly defined roles for husbands and wives. Those roles changed as our expectations of success far exceeded the income ability of the single-worker family. Two parents began working and the nuclear family lost its nucleus. This is not a statement of social judgment (whether it was right or wrong); it is merely a statement of the fragility of the nuclear family and its inability to deal with any outside pressures. In his book *New Rules: Searching for Self-Fulfillment in a World Turned Upside-Down,* sociologist, political pollster, and author Daniel Yankelovich says it like this: "It is as if tens of millions of people had decided simultaneously to conduct risky experiments in living, using the only materials that lay at hand—their own lives" (p. 1).

As the nuclear family began to fall apart, we moved into what I often term the *microwave mob.* We wash past the microwave like we are trapped in a massive tide that carries our families in multiple directions between one program and another. We connect on the fly, yelling out directions over the din of headphones donned by hurried kids as we race them off to the next event. The members of the microwave mob have very little in common—except a house—and a few shared values. Most grievous is the sense of disconnection that every member of the family feels as they cry out, "You don't understand me!" to a culture that has no time to listen.

It is the fragility of that network that is tearing our families apart not the rigors of the times in which we live.

A recent and groundbreaking study (*Hardwired to Connect: The New Scientific Case for Authoritative Communities,* A Report to the Nation from the Commission on Children at Risk) has told us that our nation faces a twofold crisis:

- The first part is a deterioration of the mental and behavioral health of U.S. children. We are witnessing high and rising rates of depression, anxiety, attention deficit, conduct disorders, thoughts of suicide, and other serious mental, emotional and behavioral problems among U.S. children and adolescents.
- The second part is how we as a society approach this deterioration. We are using medications and psychotherapies. We are designing more and more programs for special "at-risk" children. But they are not enough. Why? Because programs of individual risk-assessment and treatment seldom encourage us, and can even prevent us, from recognizing as a society the broad environmental conditions that are contributing to the growing numbers of suffering children. (pp. 5–6)

What does the report say is the cause of the crisis? "A lack of connectedness. We mean two types of connectedness—close connections to other people, and deep connections to moral and spiritual meaning" (p. 5).

The report goes on to say: "The human child is 'hardwired to connect.' We are hardwired for other people and for moral meaning and openness to the transcendent" (pp. 5–6).

How would Jesus respond to this report? What would he do? What would he tell our Church to do? It wouldn't be any different than what he spelled out to us in the Gospels over two thousand years ago. His stomach would ache over our confusion: "When he saw the crowds, he had compassion for them, because they were harassed and helpless, like sheep without a shepherd" (Matthew 9:36).

He would pray for the harvesters (people who actually go out to the harvest, as opposed to waiting in the grain elevators for the grain to harvest itself and come in): "Then he said to his disciples, 'The harvest is plentiful, but the laborers are few, therefore ask the Lord of the harvest to send out laborers into his harvest'" (Matthew 9:37–38).

He would then send us out with the authority and the power to go to the ripe fields. "Then Jesus summoned his twelve disciples and gave them authority over unclean spirits, to cast them out, and to cure every disease and every sickness" (Matthew 10:1).

And, he would commission each of us (you and me) to heal a generation, to bring a disconnected generation back into the house of the Lord. "As you go, proclaim the good news, 'The kingdom of heaven has come near.' Cure the sick, raise the dead, cleanse the lepers, cast out demons. You received without payment, give without payment" (Matthew 10:7–8).

Does that sound like your weekly to-do list?

Monday:	Proclaim the Good News, "The Kingdom is at your fingertips!"
Tuesday:	Cure the sick.
Wednesday:	Raise the dead.
Thursday:	Cast out demons.
Friday:	All other things as assigned.

Are you one of the harvesters for whom Jesus prayed? Are you leading your community into the field? Do you see the crisis of disconnectedness in our culture and, in particular among our youth, as an overwhelming problem, or do you see within it the potential for a blessed "eulogy"?

Can we hear our Lord to turn to us and say, "You feed them!" Are we ready to unlock the potential of this generation even if all we feel we can do is "mop the floor"?

It is this cauldron that will reveal the leaders of a new generation of believers.

The Potential of Church

The twofold crisis of our society represents the greatest opportunity for the Church to step into a vacuum of true need, a field ripe for the harvest. It is our grand opportunity to re-create *bayith* communities, where even the most vulnerable child can be raised in the safety and knowledge of God.

Some social commentators contend that we cannot build communities today because we cannot make commitments. However, I challenge them to see the faces of those I see every single day of my life. I challenge them to see the faces of those rejected, disenfranchised, and forgotten who excitedly proclaim, "I mopped the floor!"

Do we ask young people what we asked the kids in detention: "What type of community can we build together for your little brothers and sisters?"

Our young people are crying for communities of relevance, communities of meaning, and communities of blessing. Will we lead them by prophetic example? "Lord, show us your mop."

Communities of Blessing

Jesus speaks about a compassionate, indeed a prophetic, community in Matthew 10:40–42. He tells us that the whole point of the Church rests in four functions:

1. To be prophetic.

Prophets did not just foretell the future, they claimed it. The word itself means to forward claim as if you knew there was a treasure in a field and you sold everything to buy that treasure (see Matthew 13:34). We are prophets when we forward claim lives and even communities that others count as lost.

2. To make things right.

The word *righteousness* was almost always used in conjunction with the word *justice*, as if the two words should never be broken apart. The word wasn't about being right it was about doing right. Justice was the concept, righteousness was the action. I may desire justice, but will I work to make things right? We are most righteous when we are advocates for justice for the ones that Jesus calls in this reading, "these little ones."

3. To support those who are on the front lines of being prophetic or righteous.

We receive the prophet's reward when we house the prophets. This isn't as easy as it sounds. In Thessalonica, when the crowds couldn't find Paul, a mob of ruffians seized his host, Jason, and violently threw him before the city authorities (see Acts of the Apostles 17:5–7). These people, like Jason, not only offered their homes to the prophets and the righteous but provided them with emotional, spiritual, and financial support. They wanted the prophetic and the righteous to be out in the harvest not worrying about where their next meal was going to come from or if they would have a warm bed to lie upon at night.

To house a prophet today would be to make sure that those who are doing prophetic work (forward-claiming the lost) are supported, not just physically, but spiritually and emotionally. It is hard and grueling work to deal with such great trials day in and day out. Personally, I am grateful for those friends who know me so well that they know what I need and respond before I even have to ask.

Perhaps all of us have had a friend like that. Someone who goes beyond saying, "If you need anything, just ask." Someone who knows you so well that he or she surprises you with support before you even say anything. This person knows you need space, support, and an evening off. This is supporting the prophet—to be there without being asked—physically, emotionally, and spiritually. It is what community does.

4. To go out of our way to receive and care for the least little one that the prophetic or righteous person brings home.

Giving a cup of cold water to the littlest one would have been an unheard of act of hospitality in Christ's day. A person might have fetched cold water for a visiting dignitary or a rabbi but not a child. To fetch a cup of cold water was no easy task; it did not mean turning on the faucet and sticking a glass under it. Cold water would only come from a flowing water source, which was very hard to find in Palestine.

Is your church ready to receive the least little ones? All too often we can bring estranged young people to church with us only to find them greeted with scowls and judgment over their hairstyles or how low their pants are. How can you prepare your church to see beyond the clothes and into the needing hearts? Will your community see how much courage it took for those young people to come into a sea of unfamiliar faces and unfamiliar practices and then welcome them?

A friend of mine told me about a pastor who invited the older members of his congregation to share photographs of their grandchildren. I loved the idea and tried it in a church I was speaking to about youth issues in their community. I asked the grandparents to share their grandchildrens' photographs with one another. Then I asked them, "Do your grandchildren live in a community where a church has taken a special interest in them?"

The room became suddenly quiet after the loud and enthusiastic sharing that had just gone on. I asked them to lift up their pictures, and we prayed for those grandchildren and that some church somewhere would take a special interest in those young people's lives. Finally, I asked them if they would be willing to help me make their church a church that perhaps another grandmother or grandfather was praying for in a different city that day.

To fetch a cup of cold water today may more aptly mean reaching beyond the tough clothes, the hooded jackets, the bandanas, or the boxer shorts and extending a hand in warmth and friendship. Is your church ready to receive the least little ones? Appeal to the hearts of your church's members. Have them dig deep into their pockets—and pull out a picture of their least little one.

Jesus knew that it would take an entire community to be prophetic. It takes those who (1) "forward claim" the lost; (2) make things right when they see that things are wrong; (3) support those evangelists—the angels in the streets; and, (4) use their resources to meet the needs of the least little one. This, according to Jesus Christ, is the four-part role of *bayith,* the house of the Lord.

Does this sound like your church?

Prophetic community, *bayith* community, takes all the players. It takes a vision that is as clear as the four purposes that Jesus laid out before us. We are called to raise prophets and "right-makers," and if we are not able at this time in our lives to be out with the prophetic in the harvest, then we need to be one of those supporting the prophets or offering cold water to littlest one the prophet brings in. In other words, everyone has a role and every role is needed. Jesus lays it out so simply—this is our heritage, our call, and our Gospel challenge.

My father is an environmental scientist and a forester. We grew up with the concept of always leaving the land better off than when we found it, and that is the way that my father has lived his life. We too must ask: "Will our communities be better for our children and grandchildren because of the way that we lived? Will that be my eulogy? my blessing?"

The greatest eulogy that could ever be said about us is that we connected the little ones to community and our communities to them.

Church is one of the few places we can go today where a person could say, "I know your children by name, and you know my children by name." It is the closest thing to extended family that most families will ever experience in our very dysfunctional society. To the Hebrews, dysfunction was a focus on self at the expense of the community. Maturity meant placing self in the service of God and the people. What blessing will we impart to the youth of our cities? Will they know Jesus loved them because their community loved them?

Will your community love our children into loving? Will that be the blessing we will leave our children and our children's children? Is that . . . our beloved blessing?

Never before have the demands—and the needs—and the opportunity—for advocates and prophets to young people been so high. You may feel like the disciples at times, confronted by thousands upon thousands of the hungry and needy, but let this be your eulogy: No matter what your circumstances, no matter what your resources, you blessed them and gave them to God, and our Creator fed the entire multitude with baskets left over. Hear the words of our Lord reserved for your ears and pass them on: "This is my Son, the Beloved, with whom I am well pleased."

Here is the essence of faith simply stated by one of God's simplest servants: "I mopped the floor."

Acknowledgments

The scriptural quotations contained herein are from the New Revised Standard Version of the Bible, Catholic Edition. Copyright © 1993 and 1989 by the Division of Christian Education of the National Council of the Churches of Christ in the United States of America. All rights reserved.

The excerpts on pages 28 and 91 are from *Let the Trumpet Sound: The Life of Martin Luther King, Jr.,* by Stephen Oates (New York: Harper and Row, Publishers, 1982), pages 254–255 and 397. Copyright © 1982 by Stephen B. Oates.

The lyrics to "Hidden Statistics" on pages 69–70 are by Jerry Goebel. Copyright © 2000.

The extract on pages 75–76 is adapted from the Medstar Source story *Teen Brain,* by Medstar Television, released May 11, 2005. Used with permission of Medstar Television.

The quotation used in the author's acknowledgments and on page 80 is from *Reluctant Saint: The Life of Francis of Assisi,* by Donald Spoto (New York: Penguin Group, 2002), page 154. Copyright © 2002 by Donald Spoto.

The excerpts on pages 111–112 are from *New Testament Words: English New Testament Words Indexed with References to the Daily Study Bible,* by William Barclay (Philadelphia: Westminster Press, 1974), page 222. Copyright © 1964 by SCM Press, Ltd.

The two lists of competencies on pages 118–119 are based on *Working with Emotional Intelligence,* by Daniel Goleman (New York: Bantam Books, 1998), pages 26–27. Copyright © 1998 by Daniel Goleman.

The excerpt on page 127 is from *New Rules: Searching for Self-Fulfillment in a World Turned Upside-Down,* by Daniel Yankelovich (New York: Bantam Books, 1981), page 1. Copyright © 1981 by Daniel Yankelovich.

It is seldom that you find a book that is simultaneously profound and practical. Here it is! Jerry Goebel is offering us real wisdom and guidance for those of us who care about the next generations.

—Fr. Richard Rohr, OFM, Center for Action and Contemplation, Albuquerque, New Mexico

Here is a deeply evangelical presentation of the spiritual hungers of at-risk youth and lessons learned from years of experience and commitment.

—Dr. Michael Carotta, author of *Sometimes We Dance, Sometimes We Wrestle*

With this book, Jerry Goebel hits the mark. With a profound understanding of young people and their potential, he provides wise and compelling insight about how lives become transformed. I admire his faith in the goodness of young people and his counsel on how adults, both inside and outside the Church, can help this goodness trump hardship and our "entertain me" culture. I highly recommend this important book.

—Peter L. Benson, PhD, president and CEO, The Search Institute